Heinz Griesbach · Dora Schulz

Deutsche Sprachlehre für Ausländer

Grundstufe 2. Teil

Glossar
Deutsch-Englisch

Max Hueber Verlag

| 6. 5. 4. | Die letzten Ziffern |
| 1994 93 92 91 90 | bezeichnen Zahl und Jahr des Druckes. |

Alle Drucke dieser Auflage können, da unverändert,
nebeneinander benutzt werden.
1. Auflage
© 1979 Max Hueber Verlag, D-8045 Ismaning
Übersetzung: Joan Reutershan, New York
Satz: Brigitte Schneider, München
Druck: Druckerei Manz AG, Dillingen
Printed in the Federal Republic of Germany
ISBN 3-19-231005-7

Introduction

The language course "Deutsche Sprachlehre für Ausländer, Grundstufe, Teil II" consists of:
1. textbook
2. glossary
3. tape or cassette recordings of the lessons in the textbook.

Learning a foreign language requires a precise learning technique, if the best possible results are to be achieved. Try to examine whether or not you have already acquired an appropriate technique, that is, whether you have found the learning method most advantageous to you, and which demands the least possible amount of your time and effort.

I. Working with the text

The following procedure is recommended for working through the new texts:
1. First listen to the new text on the tape once or twice, without reading along in the textbook. Look at the pictures for the introductory text — the first text in each lesson. The pictures illustrate the individual situations in the text passage. Be sure to keep the written text in the book covered.
2. Now rewind the tape and listen to the text once again. This time read the printed text along with the tape and try to read it aloud as you follow the oral text.
3. Now rewind the tape once again, listening and reading aloud just as before. This time, however, also note with a pencil in the written text the pauses in the passage. These are clearly audible. When this has been completed for the entire text, rewind the tape and begin listening again; this time stop the tape at every pause and repeat the sentence, or sentence fragment, you have just heard. Proceed in this manner until you have completed the entire text. Always try to imitate the pronunciation and intonation exactly as you have heard them.
4. Now translate the text orally with the help of the glossary. Words which you have already learned but may have forgotten should be looked up in the dictionary. In this manner you will also learn how to work with the dictionary, and this will help you in your ongoing language study.
5. As you are working through the text, underline all the new grammar forms which have caused you difficulty in translating the text. This procedure leads into the grammar section of the lesson. Here the new grammar is explained in tables and rules. The most important grammar rules are explained in your own language in the glossary accompanying the textbook.

II. Working with the exercises

6. Before doing the exercises, try to understand the new grammar points with the aid of the tables and rules in the textbook. The grammar forms which you encountered in Part I of this language course are repeated and summarized in the first few chapters of this book. The new grammar forms complete and investigate in more detail the grammar with which you are already familiar.
7. Before you begin with the exercise, study very carefully the example sentences which introduce the exercise. A glance at the grammar terms and the tables will show you where and how the specific grammar point fits into the grammar as a whole.

8. Then complete the exercise, first orally and then in writing. If you are attending a language class, your teacher will be able to tell you whether or not you have done the exercise correctly. If you are working on your own, you can find all of the answers to the exercises in the teaching manual which accompanies this language course. Here you can check to see if you have completed all of the exercises correctly. If you have made many mistakes, repeat the exercise.

Abbreviations:
s. o. = someone
o. s. = oneself
s. th. = something
pl. = plural

ab/fertigen A: Am Schalter werden die Flugreisenden abgefertigt.
die Abfertigung, -en
ab/fliegen (o, o): Wann fliegt die Maschine ab? — Wann fliegen Sie ab?
der Abflug, ¨e
die Abflugzeit, -en
ab/heben (o, o): Die Maschine hebt jetzt vom Rollfeld ab.
die Abkürzung, -en (→ ab/kürzen A)
die Ablage, -n (→ ab/legen A): Die Ablage für die Mäntel und Jacken befindet sich über dem Fenster.
der Abschnitt, -e: Der Abschnitt des Gepäckscheins wird an das Flugticket geheftet.
allein (= anderes nicht mitgerechnet): Allein die Fahrt zum Flughafen dauert schon eine Stunde.
amtlich: Jetzt wird es noch einmal ganz amtlich.
an/fangen A (er fängt an, i, a)
der Anfänger, —
die Angabe, -n (→ an/geben A): Alle Angaben über Ihren Flug stehen auf Ihrem Flugticket.
die Anlage, -n: die elektrische Anlage
sich an/schnallen: Schnallen Sie sich bitte an! Bitte anschnallen!
der Appetit
auf/leuchten: Über dem Ausgang leuchtet jetzt unsere Flugnummer auf.
der Aufruf (→ auf/rufen A): Bis zum Aufruf unserer Maschine haben wir noch genug Zeit.
auf/rufen A (ie, u): Die Maschine wird mit der Flugnummer aufgerufen.
auf/tauchen: Während des Flugs sind keine Schwierigkeiten aufgetaucht.
der Ausgang, ¨e
aus/geben A (a, e): Wo werden die Bordkarten ausgegeben?
die Äußerung, -en
bedienen A: Die Stewardeß bedient die Passagiere an Bord.
sich befinden (a, u): Wo befinden sich hier die Parkplätze?

to clear, to check in: The flight passengers are checked in at the counter.
the clearance, the check-in
to depart (by plane), to take off: When does the plane take off? — When do you take off?
the flight departure, the take-off
the time of departure
to lift off: Now the plane lifts off from the runway.
the abbreviation
the storage compartment: The storage compartment for coats and jackets is located above the window.
the section, the claim check: The claim check of the baggage ticket is attached to the plane ticket.
alone (= other things not considered): The trip to the airport alone takes a whole hour.
official: Now things become quite official again.
to begin
the beginner
the statement, pl. the particulars, the details: All the details about your flight are on your plane ticket.
the equipment: the electrical equipment
to fasten seat belts: Please fasten your seat belts! Please fasten seat belts!
the appetite
to light up: Now our flight number lights up above the exit.
the call: We still have enough time until the call for our flight.
to call, to announce: The flight is announced by flight number.
to arise: No difficulties arose during the flight.
the exit
to give out, to hand out: Where are the boarding passes handed out?
the statement
to serve: The stewardess serves the passengers on board.
to be (found): Where is the parking lot here?

bereits = schon
already

betreten A (er betritt, a, e): Die Reisenden betreten jetzt den Flughafen.
to **enter**: Now the travelers enter the airport.

betriebsam
buzzing with activity

der **Blick**, -e: Auf der Abflugtafel kann man mit einem Blick die Abflugzeiten feststellen.
the **glance**: Departure times can be determined immediately by a glance at the departures board.

das Bodenpersonal
the ground personnel

die Bodenstewardeß, -(ss)en
the ground stewardess

Bord: an Bord gehen/sein/bleiben
board: to go on board, to be on board, to remain on board

die Bordkarte, -n
the boarding card

der Bordlautsprecher, –
the loudspeaker on board

das Brötchen, –
the roll

der **Buchstabe**, -n: Die Abkürzungen werden mit großen Buchstaben geschrieben.
the **letter**: The abbreviations are written in capital letters.

der Bus, -se
the bus

bzw. = beziehungsweise
respectively, that is

circa = ungefähr
approximately

der Code, –
the code

der Container, –
the container

da sein: Die Ablage über dem Fenster ist nur für Mäntel und Jacken da.
to **be there** (for usage): The storage compartment above the window may only be used for coats and jackets.

dabei sein: Viele Passagiere sind dabei (= darunter), die zum erstenmal fliegen.
to **be present**: Many of the passengers present (many of those among the passengers) are flying for the first time.

danach (temporal)
afterwards

dorthin: Die Reisenden werden mit dem Bus dorthin gebracht.
to **that place, there**: The passengers are brought there with the bus.

durch/sehen A (er sieht durch, a, e) = kontrollieren A
to look through = to inspect

ein/checken
to check in

eigen-: Für Sonderflüge gibt es eine eigene Abfertigung.
own, individual, separate: There is a separate check-in for special flights.

ein/sammeln A: Die Bordkarten werden wieder eingesammelt.
to **collect**: The boarding passes are collected again.

die Eisenbahn, -en
the railroad

ein/stellen A: Stellen Sie bitte das Rauchen ein! Bitte das Rauchen einstellen!
to **stop, to discontinue**: Please extinguish your cigarettes! Please extinguish cigarettes!

englisch: Wie heißt das auf englisch?
English: How do you say that in English?

erfahren (er erfährt, u. a): Was haben Sie bei der Besprechung erfahren?
to **learn, to be told**: What were you told in the conference?

erfahren: ein erfahrener Flugkapitän
experienced: an experienced flight captain

erkennen A (a, a): Haben Sie mich nicht erkannt? – Woran kann man erkennen, welcher Flug gerade abgefertigt wird?
to **recognize**: Didn't you recognize me? – How can one tell which flight is being checked in right now?

zum erstenmal
for the first time

erledigen A: Ich muß noch einige Forma- | to **settle, to take care of:** I have to take
litäten erledigen, bevor ich zu meiner | care of a few formalities before I can
Maschine gehen kann. | go to my plane.

der Fahrkartenschalter, − | the ticket counter

fast vier Millionen Flaschen Bier | almost four million bottles of beer

der Ferienreisende, -n | the vacation traveler

fest/stellen A: Wo kann man feststellen, | to **ascertain, to determine:** Where is it pos-
wann die Maschine abfliegt? | sible to determine when the flight is de-
parting?

fix und fertig verpackt | already prepared and packaged

die Fleischwaren (Plural) | the meat products

fliegen (o, o): Wir fliegen in den Urlaub. | to **fly:** We're traveling by plane on our va-
cation.

der Flug, −̈e (→ fliegen) | the flight

die Flugbesprechung, -en | the flight conference

das Flugfeld, -er | the ramp, the apron

der Fluggast, −̈e | the flight passenger

die Fluggesellschaft, -en | the airline

der Flughafen, −̈ | the airport

der Flughafenbus, -se | the airport bus

die Flughafenwelt = das Leben und Trei- | the world of the airport = life and activity
ben auf einem Flughafen | at an airport

die Flughöhe, -n | the flight altitude

der Flugingenieur, -e | the flight engineer

die Flugkarte, -n | the plane ticket

die Flugnummer, -n | the flight number

der Flugreisende, -n | the flight passenger

der Flugschein, -e | the plane ticket

das Flugticket, -s | the plane ticket

das Flugzeug, -e | the airplane

die Flugzeugbesatzung, -en | the flight crew

das Flugziel, -e | the flight destination

die **Formalität, -en:** Ich muß noch einige | the **formality:** I still have to take care of a
Formalitäten erledigen. | few formalities.

der **Fuß:** Die Maschine fliegt 18 000 Fuß | the **foot:** The plane flies at an altitude of
hoch. | 18,000 feet.

geben A (es gibt, a, e): Gleich gibt's etwas | to **be:** There will be something to eat right
zu essen. Was gibt es Gutes? | away. What's on the menu today?

sich **geben:** Das gibt sich wieder. (= Das | to **abate:** That will go away again. (= That
geht wieder vorbei.) | will pass.)

das Gefühl, -e | the feeling

genau: Das ist genau so ein Abschnitt, wie | **exactly:** That claim check is exactly like
ich ihn hier habe. | the one I have here.

das Gepäck, die Gepäckstücke | the luggage, the pieces of luggage

die Gepäckliste, -n | the baggage list

der Gepäckschein, -e | the baggage ticket

geschäftlich | business-like, on business

gespannt sein (= neugierig sein): Ich bin | to **be curious:** I wonder what there will be
gespannt, was es heute zu essen gibt. | to eat today.

gründlich | thorough(ly)

gleich (= sofort): Ich habe gleich gewußt, wo der Parkplatz ist. — **immediately, right away:** I knew right away where the parking place was.
die Halle, -n — the terminal
die **Hand:** Hand aufs Herz! (= Seien Sie ehrlich!) — the **hand:** Cross your heart! (= Be honest!)
das Handgepäck — the hand luggage
im Handumdrehen (= sehr schnell) — with a flick of the wrist (= very quickly)
heften A an A: Der Gepäckschein wird an die Flugkarte geheftet. — to **attach** s. th. to s. th.: The baggage ticket is attached to the plane ticket.
der Hinweis, -e — the hint, the tip
die Höhe, -n (→ hoch) — the altitude, the height
immer mehr: Immer mehr Menschen fliegen in den Urlaub. — **more and more:** More and more people travel by plane on their vacations.
das Instrument, -e — the instrument
der Jet, -s — the jet
die Kabine, -n — the cabin
das Kabinenpersonal — the cabin personnel
das Kinderspielzeug — children's toys
komisch (= merkwürdig) — strange (= unusual)
kontrollieren A: Das Gepäck wird kontrolliert. — to **inspect:** The baggage is inspected.
der **Kopfschmerz, -en:** Ich habe Kopfschmerzen. — the **headache:** I have a headache.
lästig sein: Wenn man Umwege machen muß, ist das immer lästig. — to **be burdensome** or **tedious:** It's tedious to go in a roundabout way.
der Lautsprecher, — — the loudspeaker
leicht: Es ist nicht leicht, sich in der Großstadt zurechtzufinden. — **easy:** It's not easy to find your way around in a large city.
die **Luft:** Die Maschine ist jetzt in der Luft. — the **air:** Now the plane is in the air.
der Magen, ¨ — the stomach
die Maschine, -n: (hier:) das Flugzeug — the machine: (here:) the airplane
melden A: Das Bodenpersonal meldet die Maschine startklar. — to **declare:** The ground personnel declares the plane ready for departure.
das Mittel, —: (hier:) das Medikament — the means: (here:) the medication
nett — nice
der Neuling, -e — the novice
das Niemandsland — no man's land
notfalls (= wenn es nötig ist) — if necessary (= if it is necessary)
nützlich — useful
das Ohr, -en: ein offenes Ohr haben (= hilfsbereit sein) — the ear: to lend an ear (= to listen and be helpful)
o. k. sein = in Ordnung sein — to be o. k. = to be in order
der Parkplatz, ¨e — the parking place; pl. the parking lot
der Paß, ¨(ss)e — the passport
die Paßkontrolle, -n — the passport control
das Problem , -e — the problem
die Quittung, -en — the receipt
der Reisende, -n — the traveler
das Reisegepäck — the luggage
die Rollbahn, -en — the runway

die Rückfahrkarte, -n
die **Ruhe**: Schauen Sie sich hier in Ruhe um.
die Sache, -n: eine scharfe hochprozentige Sache (z. B. Cognac, Whisky usw.)
der Schalter, —
schließlich
schnell: Kann ich hier schnell noch mal telefonieren?
sehen: Na, sehen Sie! (hier: Ich habe das vorausgesehen.)
der Service
servieren: Die Stewardeß serviert jetzt das Essen.
der Sonderflug, ⁼e
der Sonntagsausflug, ⁼e
sparen A: Wenn Sie diese Straße fahren, sparen Sie Umwege.
der Start, -s
starten A: Die Maschine startet. Der Pilot startet die Maschine.
startklar
stehen (a, a): Auf dem Wegweiser steht das Wort „Abflüge".
der Steward, -s
die Stewardeß, -(ss)en
der Tank, -s
das Tor, -e: das Tor zur großen weiten Welt
der Transitraum, ⁼e
sich **treffen** (er trifft, a, o): Wir treffen uns zu einer Besprechung.
das Triebwerk, -e
der **Tropfen**, —: ein guter Tropfen (hier:) = ein guter Wein
tüchtig
sich **um/schauen** (= sich orientieren): Ich schaue mich jetzt hier in Ruhe um.

um/steigen (ie, ie): Ich muß in Frankfurt umsteigen.
um/tauschen A: Wo kann man hier Geld umtauschen?
der Umweg, -e
unverzollt: unverzollte Zigaretten
der Urlaub, -e
sich **vergewissern** G: Haben Sie sich schon vergewissert, wann Ihre Maschine abfliegt?

the round-trip ticket
peace and quiet: Look around here as long as you like.
the thing: a strong substance of high alcoholic content (i. e., cognac, whiskey)
the counter
finally
quick, quickly: Can I still make a quick phone call here?
to **see**: There, you see! (here: I anticipated that.)
the service
to **serve**: Now the stewardess serves the meal.
the special flight
the Sunday outing
to **save, to spare**: If you take this road, you'll spare unnecessary driving.
the start, the take-off
to **start, to take off**: The plane takes off. The pilot starts the engines.
ready for departure
to **stand, to be**: The word "departures" is on the signboard.
the steward
the stewardess
the tank
the gate: the gate to the big wide world
the transit lounge
to **meet**: We meet for a conference.
the engines, the transmission
the **drop**: a good drink (here:) a good wine
efficient
to **look around** (to find one's bearings): Now I'm going to look around here as long as I like.
to **transfer**: I have to transfer in Frankfurt.
to **change**: Where can one change money here?
the roundabout way, the detour
duty-free: duty-free cigarettes
the vacation
to **ascertain, to confirm**: Have you already confirmed when your flight is departing?

verlassen A (er verläßt, ie, a): Die Passagiere werden gebeten, die Maschine zu verlassen.

to leave, to deplane: The passengers are requested to deplane.

sich versammeln: Vor dem Flug versammelt sich die Flugzeugbesatzung zu einer Besprechung.

to gather, to get together: Before the flight the crew gathers for a conference.

verschieden = unterschiedlich

various = different

der Vorfeldbus, -se

the ramp bus

vorher

before, beforehand

die Waage, -n

the scale

die Wahl treffen (= wählen): Hast du bei deinem Einkauf auch die richtige Wahl getroffen?

to make a choice (= choose): Did you really make the right choice with your purchase?

der Wegweiser, —

the signpost, the signboard

weiter/fliegen (o, o): Wann fliegt unsere Maschine weiter?

to continue the flight: When does our flight continue?

das Wetter

the weather

wichtig sein: Die Reise ist für mich sehr wichtig.

to be important: This trip is very important for me.

wiegen A (o, o): Hier wird das Gepäck gewogen.

to weigh: The luggage is weighed here.

wissen (er weiß, wußte, hat gewußt)

to know

das Wunder, —: Kein Wunder! (= Man braucht sich nicht zu wendern.)

the marvel, the wonder: No wonder! (= One need not be surprised.)

die Wurstwaren (Plural)

sausage products

zeigen A: Er will nicht zeigen, daß er ein Anfänger ist.

to show: He doesn't want to show that he's a beginner.

die Zollkontrolle, -n

customs inspection

zu/gehen (i, a): Auf den Flughäfen geht es immer sehr betriebsam zu!

to happen, to take place: Airports are always buzzing with activity.

zu/greifen (i, i): Die hungrigen Passagiere greifen (beim Essen) tüchtig zu.

to take hold of: The hungry passengers dig in (to the meal) heartily.

sich zurecht/finden (a, u): In dieser Stadt finde ich mich gut zurecht.

to get along, to find one's way around: I'm finding my way around this city well.

zusammen/stellen A: Wir haben hier einige nützliche Hinweise zusammengestellt.

to compile: We've compiled a few useful tips here.

zusätzlich

additional, additionally

zuvor = vorher

first (= beforehand)

die Zwischenlandung, -en

the stopover

Abschnitt 2

ab/springen (a, u): Von einer fahrenden Bahn darf man nicht abspringen.

to jump off: It's not permitted to jump off a moving train.

der Acht-Stunden-Tag: ein Arbeitstag von acht Stunden Arbeitszeit (vgl. die 40-stunden-Woche)

the eight-hour day: a workday consisting of eight hours worktime (compare: the forty-hour week) also doch (= es ist also doch so, wie ich es mir vorher gedacht habe)

after all: It's just like I had imagined it after all.

amtlich

official

sich **an/schaffen** A: Mein Mann hat sich eine Stereo-Anlage angeschafft.

to **purchase:** My husband bought himself a stereo set.

an/gehen A (i, a): Niemanden geht es etwas an, was ich hier tue.

to **concern:** What I do here concerns no one.

an/sehen A (er sieht an, a, e): Er sieht das Mädchen an. — Ich sehe die Angelegenheit als nicht so wichtig an.

to **look at, to regard:** He looks at the girl. — I don't regard the matter as so important.

an/setzen A: Meine Frau will heute eine Bowle ansetzen.

to **prepare:** My wife wants to prepare a punch today.

an/sprechen A (er spricht an, a, o): Heute hat mich auf der Straße ein Mann angesprochen.

to **address, to speak to:** Today a man spoke to me on the street.

auf/füllen A: Jetzt mußt du die Bowle mit Sekt auffüllen.

to **fill up:** Now you have to fill up the punch bowl with champagne.

auf/geben A (er gibt auf, a, e): Meine Frau will ihren Beruf jetzt aufgeben.

to **surrender, to give up:** Now my wife wants to give up her career.

automatisch

automatic(ally)

aus sein (= vorbei sein): Jetzt ist es mit der Liebe aus.

to **be over (to be past):** The romance is over now.

sich **aus/wirken** auf A: Was wirkt sich auf die Männer psychisch aus?

to **have an effect upon:** What has a psychological effect on men?

backen A: Meine Frau will heute eine Torte backen.

to **bake:** My wife wants to bake a pie today.

die Bahn, -en (hier: die Straßenbahn)

the train (here: the streetcar)

beachten A: Haben Sie auch die Neuregelung des Gesetzes beachtet?

to **heed, to pay attention to:** Have you paid attention to the new specifications of the law?

bedauern A: Ich bedauere dich. - Ich bedauere, daß ich gestern nicht kommen konnte. — Sie sagte es bedauernd.

to **regret, to pity:** I'm sorry for you. — I regret that I wasn't able to come yesterday. — She said it regretfully.

der Begriff, -e

the concept, the idea

begrüßen A: Die Öffentlichkeit begrüßte die Neuregelung des Gesetzes.

to **greet, to welcome:** The public welcomes the revision of the law.

die Behörde, -n

the (administrative) authorities

besagen: Das neue Gesetz besagt, ...

to **say, to state:** The new law states ...

blöd: Es ist zu blöd, daß du morgen nicht kommen kannst.

stupid, ridiculous: It's really just idiotic that you can't come tomorrow.

bloß (= nur): Was hast du gestern bloß gemacht?

merely (= only): Just what exactly did you do yesterday?

das Blumenbild, -er

the picture of flowers

die Bowle, -n

the punch bowl, the punch

das **Büfett, -s:** Meine Frau hat für die Gäste ein kaltes Büfett vorbereitet.

the **buffet dinner:** My wife prepared a cold buffet dinner for the guests.

dabei sein: Bei seiner Freude war auch etwas Enttäuschung dabei.

to **be there:** A bit of disappointment was mixed with his joy.

damals

at that time

dramatisch

dramatic, dramatcially

das **Ding**: Mein Mann hat sich so ein teures Ding von Stereo-Anlage gekauft.

the **thing**: My husband bought himself some expensive stereo set.

dumm: Es ist zu dumm, daß wir uns morgen nicht treffen können.

dumb: It's really just ridiculous that we can't meet tomorrow.

die Ehefrau, -en
der Ehemann, ⸚er
die Eheschließung, -en (→ eine Ehe schließen)

the wife
the husband
the marriage

eigentlich: Wie lange seid ihr eigentlich schon verheiratet?

real(ly), actual(ly): How long have you actually been married already?

einfach

simple, simply

ein/richten A: Wir haben unsere Wohnung neu eingerichtet.

to **arrange, to furnish**: We've refurnished our apartment.

die Emanzipation
emanzipiert

the emancipation
emancipated

sich **entschließen** zu (o, o): Wozu habt ihr euch jetzt entschlossen?

to **decide to**: What have you decided to do now?

entschuldigen A: Entschuldige, daß ich danach gefragt habe.

to **excuse**: Excuse my asking about it.

die Enttäuschung, -en (→ enttäuschen A)

the disappointment

ergreifen A (i, i): Wann willst du endlich einmal die Initiative ergreifen? (Wann willst du endlich einmal etwas dafür/dagegen tun?)

to **take hold of**: When do you finally intend to take the initiative? (When do you finally intend to do something about it?)

erhalten A (er erhält, ie, a): Die junge Ehefrau erhält den Familiennamen des Ehemannes.

to **receive**: The young wife receives the family name of the husband.

erraten A (er errät, ie, a): Du errätst nicht, wer gestern bei uns war.

to **guess**: You'll never guess who was at our place yesterday.

erstaunt (→ erstaunen)

astonished

erwarten A: Die junge Frau erwartet ein Kind.

to **expect**: The young woman expects a child.

erweitern A = vergrößern A
die Existenzgrundlage, -n
der Fall, ⸚e: in diesem Fall

to enlarge = to increase
the main source of income
the case: in this case

fertig sein (= zu Ende sein): Ende des Jahres bin ich mit meinem Studium fertig.

to **be finished**: At the end of the year I'll be finished with my academic studies.

der Fortbestand (→ fort/bestehen): der Fortbestand des Familiennamens

the continuation, the endurance: the continuation of the family name

die **Freude**: Gudrun hat viel Freude an Gesprächen.

the **joy**: Gudrun enjoys conversation very much.

freudig
früh = frühzeitig
ganz nett, ganz normal
gar nicht

joyful(ly)
early
quite nice, quite normal
not at all

geboren (Partizip Perfekt): Frau Schmidt, geborene Müller

born: Mrs. Schmidt, née Müller

der Geburtsname, -n = Mädchenname

maiden name

es **geht** (i, a): So gut, wie ihr denkt, geht es uns nun auch wieder nicht.

things are going: Things aren't really going quite as well for us as you think.

gelingen D (a, u): Das war gestern wirklich ein gelungener Abend.

to be a success: That was really a successful evening yesterday.

der Gemüsesalat, -e

the vegetable salad

die Genehmigung, -en (→ genehmigen A)

the permit, the permission

die Geschichte (= die Sache): Die Geschichte ist gar nicht so dramatisch.

the story (= the matter): The story is not so dramatic at all.

gutaussehend: ein gutaussehender Mann

good-looking: a good-looking man

die Haltestelle, -n

the stop

der Haushalt: Meine Frau führt den Haushalt allein. — Die Kosten des Haushalts steigen ständig.

the household: My wife runs the household by herself. Household expenses keep increasing.

das Hemd, -en

the shirt

heran/schaffen A: Ich muß das Geld für den Haushalt heranschaffen.

to procure, to provide: I have to provide money for the household.

die Industrie, -n

the industry

die Initiative, -n

the initiative

sich interessieren für: Ich interessiere mich für Musik.

to be interested in: I am interested in music.

der Jahrgang, ¨-e: Mein Mann ist Jahrgang 1947.

year of birth, of graduation, of publication, of productions: 1947 was the year of my husband's birth.

der Job, -s

the job

der Junge, -n (hier: der junge Mann)

the boy (here: the young man)

der Jurist, -en

the lawyer

kariert: ein kariertes Hemd

checked: a checked shirt

die Kosten (Plural): Wer trägt die Kosten für den Haushalt?

the costs: Who assumes the household expenses?

der Krach, ¨-e: Gestern hatte ich wieder einmal Krach mit meinem Mann.

the noise, the quarrel: Yesterday I had an argument with my husband again.

in Kraft treten (es tritt in Kraft, a, e): Mit dem 1. Juli ist ein neues Gesetz in Kraft getreten.

to come into power: On July 1st a new law came into force.

die Krankenschwester, -n

the nurse

lächeln

to smile

lebhaft: Das Bild war in lebhaften Farben gemalt.

lively: The picture was painted with lively colours.

der Mädchenname, -n

the maiden name

malen A: Sie malt gern Blumenbilder.

to paint: She likes to paint pictures of flowers.

der Mann, ¨-er (= der Ehemann, ¨-er): mein Mann

the man (= the husband): my husband

der Mediziner, —

the medical man, student of medicine

mehrmals

often

meinen: Ich habe das nicht so gemeint. (als Entschuldigung)

to mean: I didn't mean it that way. (as apology)

die Melone, -n

the melon

messen: An ihm gemessen kommt sie sich klein vor. (= Im Vergleich zu ihm kommt sie sich klein vor.)

to measure: Compared to him she considers herself short.

die Miete, -n

the rent

mißlingen D (a, u): Die Torte ist mir leider mißlungen.

to fail: Unfortunately my pie was a failure.

nach/lächeln D: Als der junge Mann weiterging, lächelte sie ihm nach.

to smile after s. o.: She smiled after the young man as he continued on his way.

nach/schauen D: Der junge Mann schaute dem Mädchen nach.

to gaze after: The youn man gazed after the girl.

das Namengesetz, -e

the law regarding names

nennen (a, a): Man nennt Peter einen gutaussehenden Mann.

to name, to call: Peter is considered a good-looking man.

die Neuregelung, -en (→ etwas neu regeln): die Neuregelung des Gesetzes

the rearrangement, the revision: the revision of the law

das Objekt, -e: Alle Personen oder Sachen, die das im Satz beschriebene Geschehen betrifft, werden im Satz als Objekte genannt. (Vgl. auch Subjekt)

the object: Objects are all those persons or things which are affected by the event described in the sentence.

der Obstsalat, -e

the fruit salad

offen sein (= noch nicht klar sein): Das Problem ist noch offen.

to be open (= to be not yet clear): The problem is not yet clear.

die Öffentlichkeit: Sie liebt die Öffentlichkeit.

the public: She loves the public.

das Paar, -e: das junge Paar

the couple: the young couple

die Pharmazie

the pharmacy

psychisch

psychological(ly)

räumen A (= leer machen): Das kalte Büfett war schon nach kurzer Zeit geräumt.

to clear away (to empty): In just a little while the cold buffet dinner had disappeared.

die Rechtswissenschaft, -en

jurisprudence

rechtzeitig: Wir sind noch rechtzeitig zum Zug gekommen.

on time: We still arrived on time for the train.

die Rede: Das Problem ist nicht der Rede wert.

the talk: The problem isn't worth talking about.

der Reissalat, -e

the rice salad

schlank: eine schlanke, junge Frau

slim: a slender, young woman

die Schreibkraft, ⸚e = der/die Büroangestellte

the secretary = the office employee

der Schritt, -e: Auf dem Weg zur Emanzipation der Frau sind wir einen großen Schritt weitergekommen.

the step: We've gone one large step further in the direction of women's emancipation.

die Sekretärin, -nen

the secretary

die Sekunde, -n: in letzter Sekunde

the second: in the last second

der Sekt

the sparkling wine, the champagne

das Semester, —

the semester

signalisieren A: Die Kasusformen signalisieren, welche Funktion die Nomen oder Pronomen im Satz haben und wovon sie abhängen.

to signal, to indicate: The cases indicate what function the nouns and pronouns have in the sentence and how they are related to other parts of the sentence.

sozusagen

so to say, so to speak

zu spät kommen

to come too late

die Stereo-Anlage, -n

the stereo set

das Subjekt: Im Subjekt eines Satzes wird

the subject: The subject of the sentence

die Person oder Sache genannt, über die etwas mitgeteilt wird. Das Subjekt des Satzes erkennt man an der Nominativform.

indicates the person or thing about whom or which something is said. The subject of the sentence can be recognized because it is in the nominative case.

sorgen für: Mein Sohn wird für den Fortbestand unseres Familiennamens sorgen.

to **take care of, to see to:** My son will see to the continuation of our family name.

der **Stammhalter,** — = der Sohn einer Familie

the **eldest son and heir in a family**

der Textil-Großhandel

the wholesale textile trade

die Torte, -n: Schwarzwälder Torte

the pie or cake: Black Forest cake

tragen A (er trägt, u, a): Wer trägt bei euch die Kosten für den Haushalt?

to **carry, to assume:** Who in your family assumes the household expenses?

übrig: im übrigen

(left)over: by the way

der **Umgang:** Sie liebt den Umgang mit jungen Menschen.

the **association:** She loves to associate with young people.

ungut: nichts für ungut (als Entschuldigung)

amiss: No harm meant (as apology)

die Uni, -s = die Universität, -en

the university

ursprünglich

original(ly)

die Vergangenheit (als Zeitabschnitt)

the past (as time unit)

verheiratet

married

das Verlagshaus, ⁻er

the publishing house

der Vermessungsingenieur, -e

the survey engineer

sich **vor/kommen:** Sie kommt sich an ihm gemessen klein vor.

to **seem, to appear:** She considers herself short compared to him.

die **Wahl:** Die Pullover, die ich gekauft habe, sind nur 2. Wahl. — Wir haben die Wahl zwischen zwei Möglichkeiten.

the **choice:** The sweaters I bought are only seconds. — We have the choice between two possibilities.

wählen: Wir können nur zwischen zwei Möglichkeiten wählen.

to **choose:** We can only choose between two possibilities.

das **Weinjahr, -e:** 1975 war ein gutes Weinjahr.

the **vintage year:** 1975 was a good vintage year.

weiter/gehen (i, a): Erzähle, wie die Geschichte weitergegangen ist!

to **continue, to go on:** Tell how the story went on!

wiederum = andererseits

on the other hand = on the contrary

zucken: Sie antwortete nicht, sondern zuckte nur mit den Schultern.

to **shrug:** She didn't answer, but only shrugged her shoulders.

zurück/lächeln: Er lächelte sie an, und sie lächelte zurück.

to **smile back:** He smiled at her and she smiled back.

Abschnitt 3

ab/lehnen A: Er lehnt das Angebot ab.

to **decline:** He is declining the offer.

die Alpen

the Alps

das Angebot, -e (→ an/bieten A)

the offer

annähernd (= ungefähr)

nearly (= approximately)

die **Annahme** (→ an/nehmen A): Er verweigert die Annahme des Briefes.

the **acceptance**: He refuses to accept the letter.

das **Attribut**, -e: Attribute sind Wörter, die Personen, Sachen oder Begriffe klassifizieren oder identifizieren.

the **attribute**: Attributes are words which classify or identify persons, things or ideas.

aus/richten D + A (= sagen D + A): Ich soll Ihnen Grüße von Herrn Schmidt ausrichten.

to **deliver** (a message) = to tell s. o. s. th.: I'm supposed to convey kind regards to you from Mr. Schmidt.

außer Haus sein = nicht im Hause sein

to be out of the office = to be not in the office

außerhalb: Ich rufe von außerhalb an.

outside: I'm calling from outside.

ausschließlich = nur

exclusively = only

Bahn: Die Waren werden per Bahn transportiert.

rail: The goods are conveyed by rail.

die Banane, -n

the banana

bayerisch

Bavarian

behaupten A: Er behauptet: ,,Ich habe die Ware nicht bestellt."

to **maintain**: He maintains, "I did not order the merchandise".

es sich **bequem machen:** Er machte es sich hier bei uns bequem.

to **make o. s. comfortable:** He made himself comfortable at our place.

bereit sein: Sind Sie bereit, das Tier zu verkaufen?

to **be prepared:** Are you prepared to sell the animal?

bereits = schon

already

bestellen A: Wir haben bei der Firma Waren bestellt.

to **order:** We've ordered merchandise from the company.

bestellen D + A: Bestellen Sie bitte Herrn Schmidt, daß wir angerufen haben.

to **leave s. o. a message:** Please leave Mr. Schmidt a message that we called.

der Bestimmungshafen, ⸚

the port of destination

der Bestimmungsort, -e

the place of destination

betragen (er beträgt, u, a): Wieviel betragen die Transportkosten?

to **amount to, to come to:** How much do the shipping costs amount to?

der Bewohner, —

the inhabitant

bis zu: Der Elefant verlangt täglich bis zu 15 Kilo Bananen.

up to: The elephant demands up to 15 kilograms of bananas daily.

bislang = bis jetzt

until now

die Box, -en

the compartment

chinesisch

Chinese

da sein = hier sein

to be present = to be here

darunter (hier: unter diesen Sprachen)

among them (here: among these languages)

deutschsprachig: deutschsprachige Gebiete (= Gebiete, in denen die Bewohner deutsch sprechen)

German-speaking: German-speaking regions (= areas in which the inhabitants speak German)

der Dialekt, -e

the dialect

der Dialektausdruck, ⸚e

the dialect expression

der Dickhäuter, —

the pachyderm

eher = lieber

rather = preferably

ein/treffen (er trifft ein, a, o): Sind die Waren aus Bangkok schon eingetroffen?

to **arrive:** Has the merchandise from Bangkok arrived already?

der Elefant, -en

the elephant

der Elefantenbulle, -n

the elephant bull

der **Empfang:** In Empfang nehmen: Wer nimmt die Waren in Empfang?

der Empfänger, — (→ empfangen)

endgültig

die Entscheidung, -en (→ entscheiden A)

der Erdenbewohner, — = der Mensch

erreichbar sein: Wann ist Herr Schmidt zu Hause erreichbar?

erreichen A: Wann kann ich Sie (telefonisch) erreichen?

der Exporteur, -e

das Ferngespräch, -e

fernöstlich

die Flasche, -n

die Flüssigkeit, -en (→ flüssig)

das Frachtschiff, -e

frei/geben A (er gibt frei, a, e): Das Tier wurde zum Verkauf freigegeben.

sich fühlen: Er fühlt sich hier sitzengelassen.

furchtbar (hier: sehr)

das Gebiet, -e

gelten (er gilt, a, o): Das gilt besonders für das Niederdeutsche.

sich gewöhnen an A: Er hat sich an das Klima gewöhnt.

gleichen D (i, i): Kein Dialekt gleicht genau der Schriftsprache.

die Grenze, -n

der Hafen, ⸺

heißen: das heißt ... (d. h.)

das Heu

die Holzkiste, -n

der Hoteldiener, —

der Importeur, -e

indessen = inzwischen

die Intonation

jedenfalls = auf jeden Fall

jeweils

Jumbo (hier: der Elefant)

der Karton, -s

der Kellerraum, ⸺e

die Kiste, -n

komisch

der Lastwagen, —

leben: die lebende Sprache

liefern D + A: Wann können Sie uns die Ware liefern?

---

the reception, the receipt: to receive: Who signs for the merchandise?

the recipient, the addressee

final(ly)

the decision

the inhabitant of the earth = human being

to **be reachable:** When can Mr. Schmidt be reached at home?

to **reach:** When can I reach you (by telephone)?

the exporter

the long distance call

far eastern

the bottle

the fluid, the liquid

the freighter

to **release:** The animal was released for sale.

to **feel:** He feels left in the lurch here.

terribly = very

the area, the region

to **be valid, or true:** That is especially true for Low German.

to **become accustomed to:** He has become accustomed to the climate.

to **equal, to be like:** No dialect is precisely like the written language.

the border

the port

to **be called; to mean or signify:** that means (to say) ... (i. e.)

the hay

the wooden crate

the hotel attendant

the importer

meanwhile = in the meantime

the intonation

in any case

respectively, each

Jumbo (here: the elephant)

the carton

the basement area

the box, the crate

strange

the truck

to live: the living language

to **deliver:** When can you deliver the merchandise to us?

der Lkw, -s (→ der Lastkraftwagen, −) — the freight truck

die **Luftfracht, -en:** Die Waren werden als Luftfracht transportiert. — the **air freight:** The products are shipped as air freight.

mal eben (= so nebenbei) — just

manch-: Hier ist manches schon passiert. — **many:** Many things have happened here already.

die Menge, -n: große/kleine Mengen — the quantity: large/small quantities

die Muttersprache, -n — the mother tongue

neben = außer — beside(s)

nehmen (er nimmt, a, o): ein Bad nehmen — to take: to take a bath

neulich = vor einiger Zeit — recently: a short time ago

niederdeutsch — Low German

die Nordseeküste, -n — the coast of the North Sea

der Notverkauf, "-e (= ein Verkauf wegen einer Notlage) — the emergency sale (= a sale because of an emergency)

die Nummer, -n (hier: die Telefonnummer) — the number (here: the telephone number)

offensichtlich — obvious(ly), apparent(ly)

passieren: Hier ist manches schon passiert. — to **take place, to happen:** Many things have happened here already.

der Raum, "-e (hier: das Gebiet, -e) — the room, the area (here: the region)

die Rückfrage, -n (→ zurück/fragen) — the query

rund = ungefähr — around = approximately

russisch — Russian

der Sack, "-e — the sack

scheiden sehen: Er sieht das Tier ungern scheiden. (= Er möchte sich nicht gern von dem Tier trennen.) — to **see (s. o., s. th.) leave:** He doesn't like to see the animal leave. (= He doesn't want to be separated from the animal.)

das **Schicksal, -e:** Man hat sich über das weitere Schicksal des Tieres noch nicht entschieden. — the **destiny, the fate:** The animal's future lot has not yet been decided.

das **Schiff, -e:** Die Waren werden per Schiff transportiert. — the **ship:** The goods are conveyed by ship.

die Schriftsprache, -n — the written language

Schwierigkeit: Schwierigkeiten bereiten: Dialekte bereiten den ausländischen Schülern Schwierigkeiten. — **difficulty:** to cause difficulties: Dialects cause difficulties for foreign students of German.

nicht selten (= oft) — not infrequently = often

der Skorpion, -e — the scorpion

Spaß haben an + D: Wir haben viel Spaß an dem Tier. — to **enjoy:** We enjoy the animal very much.

Spitze: an der Spitze stehen (= der/das/die erste sein) — the point, the top: to be on the top (= to be the first)

das Sprachgebiet, -e — the language area or region

die Sprechweise, -n — the manner of speaking

stammen aus: Er stammt aus Hamburg. — to **originate from, to come from:** He comes from Hamburg.

stark: nicht so stark (= nicht so sehr) — great(ly): not so intensely, not to such a great extent (= not so much)

der Tank, -s — the tank

der Tankwagen, − — the tank truck

Telex: per Telex (= per Fernschreiben)	telex: by telex (= by teletype)
die Tiefebene, -n	the lowland(s)
das Tier, -e	the animal
der Tierhändler, –	the animal dealer
der Tierkeller, – (= ein Keller, in dem Tiere gehalten werden)	the animal cellar (= a cellar in which animals are kept)
der Tiger, –	the tiger
die Tonne, -n	the cask
der Torf	the peat
das Torfbad: ein Torfbad nehmen (= sich im Torf wälzen)	the peat bath: to take a peat bath (= to roll in peat)
der Transport, -e	the transport, the shipment, the conveyance
transportieren A	to ship, to convey, to transport
das Transportmittel, –	the means of conveyance
um/laden A (er lädt um, u, a): Die Waren werden auf Lkws umgeladen.	to transfer: The products are transferred onto freight trucks.
um/schlagen A (er schlägt um, u, a): Am Hafen werden die Waren umgeschlagen.	to reship: The products are reshipped at the port.
ungern (= nicht gern)	reluctantly = not gladly
unterscheiden A (ie, ie): Man unterscheidet drei Dialektgruppen.	to distinguish, to differentiate: Three dialect groups can be distinguished.
der Unterschied, -e	the difference
verladen A (er verlädt, u, a): Hier werden die Waren auf Frachtschiffe verladen.	to load: Here the goods are loaded onto freighters.
verlangen A: Was verlangen Sie von mir? – Die Firma verlangt für den Transport 1 400 Dollar.	to demand, to charge: What are you going to charge me? – The company is charging 1,400 dollars for shipment.
verpacken A: Die Waren werden in Kisten verpackt.	to pack: The goods are packed in crates.
verreist sein: Herr Birnbaum ist verreist.	to be out of town: Mr. Birnbaum is out of town.
versorgen A: Er versorgt täglich die Tiere.	to take care of, to look after: He tends to the animals daily.
versuchen A (= probieren A)	to try
verweigern A: Er verweigert die Annahme des Briefes.	to refuse: He refuses to accept the letter.
vielfach (= oft, häufig)	in many cases = often, frequently
vollklimatisiert	fully air-conditioned
vorhin = vor kurzer Zeit	before = a short time ago
vor/liegen (a, e)= vorhanden sein: Es liegen schon einige Angebote vor.	to be under consideration = to be present: Several offers are being considered.
die Vorwahl(nummer, -n) = Ortsnummer beim Telefon	the area code = area code for telephoning
die Ware, -n	the product, the commodity; pl. goods, merchandise
Wasser: Die waren werden zu Wasser transportiert.	the water: The goods are conveyed by water.
Weg: in die Wege leiten: Wir haben den Verkauf bereits in die Wege geleitet.	the way, the direction; to arrange for: We've already arranged for the sale.

weiter-: Er verlangt für den Transport noch weitere 1 400 Dollar.

die Wissenschaft, -en

der Wochenanfang

die Zahlung, -en (→ zahlen)

der Zentner (= 50 Kilogramm)

der Zoologe, -n

die Zwangseinquartierung, -en (→ zwangsweise einquartieren)

further, additional: He is charging yet an additional 1,400 dollars for shipment.

the science

the beginning of the week

the hundredweight

the zoologist

the forced quartering

Abschnitt 4

das Abgangszeugnis, -se

der Abschluß → ab/schließen (Schule)

das Abschlußzeugnis, -se

abschüssig: eine abschüssige Straße

ab/springen (a, u): Die Schüler sprangen vom Wagen ab.

Achtung!

das Alter: im Alter von sechs Jahren

altsprachlich: ein altsprachliches Gymnasium

ander-: unter anderem

der Anlaß, ‼(ss)e

der Anlasser, —

der Applaus

das Aufbaugymnasium, -gymnasien

the school-leaving certificate

the completion: to finish school

the certificate of completion, the diploma

precipitous: a steep street

to **jump off:** The school children jumped from the car.

Attention!

the age: at six years of age

of classical languages: a high school emphasizing classical languages

other: among other things

the cause

the starter

the applause

the equivalency high school, leading to the *Abitur* (university admission diploma)

auf/passen auf A: Passen Sie auf den Verkehr auf!

aufregend: ein aufregendes Erlebnis

aus/scheiden (ie, ie): Er ist aus der Schule ausgeschieden.

die Auszeichnung, -en (→ aus/zeichnen A)

die Automatik

das Bad, ‼er (hier: das Hallenbad)

beglückwünschen A: Man beglückwünschte mich zu der Auszeichnung.

bei/legen A + D: Ich lege den Zeitungsausschnitt dem Brief bei.

bereit/stehen (a, a): Der Bus steht schon bereit.

die Berufsausbildung, -en

die Berufsschule, -n

betätigen A: Betätigen Sie jetzt den Anlasser!

to **pay attention to:** Do watch out for the traffic!

exciting: an exciting experience

to **leave, to withdraw:** He withdrew from school.

the distinction

the automatic transmission

the bath, the pool: (here: indoor pool)

to **congratulate:** I was congratulated for the distinction.

to **enclose:** I'm enclosing the newspaper clipping in the letter.

to **be ready, to be waiting:** The bus is waiting already.

the vocational training

the vocational school

to **set in motion, to activate:** Now activate the starter!

bewahren A vor: Sie bewahrte ihre Mitschüler vor schweren Verletzungen.

to **protect:** She protected her schoolmates
from serious injuries.

bezeichnen A als: Er bezeichnete die Tat
als leuchtendes Beispiel für mutiges Verhalten.

to **designate:** He designated the deed as a
shining example of courageous behavior.

der **Blinker,** —: Was ist denn mit dem Blinker? (= Warum betätigen Sie den Blinker nicht?)

the **blinker:** What's the problem with the
blinker? (Why aren't you using the
blinker?)

die Bordsteinkante, -n

the curb

die Bremse, -n

the brake

bremsen

to brake

das Bremspedal, -e

the brake pedal

der Busfahrer, —

the bus driver

damals

at that time

die Ehrenurkunde, -n

the certificate of honor

die Ehrung, -en (→ ehren A)

the honors ceremony

ein/biegen (o, o): Der Wagen biegt nach
rechts in die Straße ein.

to **turn:** The car is turning to the right into
the street.

einfach = nur

simply = only

ein/legen A: Legen Sie jetzt den 1. Gang
ein!

to **shift:** Now shift into first gear.

ein/parken: Ich parke meinen Wagen jetzt
hier ein.

to **parallel park:** I'm (parallel) parking my
car here.

ein/schlagen (er schlägt ein, u, a): Schla-
gen Sie jetzt das Steuer/die Räder
rechts ein!

to **turn:** Now turn the steering wheel/the
wheels to the right.

einstimmig

unanimously

ein/treten (er tritt ein, a, e): Er tritt jetzt
in die Schule ein.

to **enter:** He's entering school now.

einzig: als einziger/einziges/einzige

only: as the only (one) (masculine, neuter,
feminine)

enden mit: Die Schule endet mit der 10.
Klasse.

to **end** (after): The school ends after the
tenth grade.

die Entfernung, -en

the distance

entgegen/nehmen A (er nimmt entgegen,
a, o): Sie hat ihre Urkunde entgegenge-
nommen.

to **accept, to receive:** She accepted her
certificate.

sich **entschließen** zu (o, o): Sie hat sich zu
einer mutigen Tag entschlossen.

to **decide:** She decided to do a courageous
deed.

erfolglos

in vain

das Erlebnis, -se

experience, event

ermöglichen (= möglich machen): Er er-
möglichte seinem Sohn ein Studium an
der Universität.

to **enable:** He made it possible for his son
to study at a university.

erreichen A: Er hat das 7. Lebensjahr erreicht.

to **reach:** He has reached his seventh year.

die Fachschule, -n

the technical school

der Fahrerseitz, -e

the driver's seat

der Fahrgastraum, ̈-e

the passenger area

die Fahrschule, -n

the driving school

das Fahrzeug, -e	the vehicle
die Feier, -n	the celebration
die Förderstufe, -n	the special preparations class (for transfer to a higher level school)
sich **freuen**: Sie freut sich.	to **be happy**: She is happy.
führerlos: ein führerloses Auto	driverless: a driverless car
der Fußgänger, –	the pedestrian
der Gang, ⁻e (beim Auto)	the gear (in a car)
Gang: in Gang setzen: Er setzt den Motor in Gang.	**motion**: to set in motion: He gets the motor going.
die Garage, -n	the garage
Gas geben (er gibt Gas, a, e): Geben Sie nicht so viel Gas!	to **give gas**: Don't give so much gas!
gefährlich	dangerous
gehen (i, a): Das geht ja ganz gut (= Das machen Sie ja ganz gut.)	to **go**: That's going very well. (= You're really doing that very well.)
gehoben: der gehobene Dienst (bei Behörden)	elevated: upper-level employment (in administration)
geradeaus	straight ahead
gesamt: die gesamte Schule	entire: the entire school
die Gesichtsverletzung, -en	the facial injury
gleich/stehen D: Die Mittlere Reife steht der Fachschulreife gleich.	to **be equivalent to:** The intermediate high school diploma is equivalent to the technical school diploma.
der Grund, ⁻e	the reason
grundsätzlich	basic, basically
das Gymnasium, die Gymnasien	the preparatory high school, leading to the *Abitur* (the university admission diploma)
das Hallenbad, ⁻er	the indoor pool
die **Hand**: sich die Hand brechen: Ein Schüler hat sich die Hand gebrochen.	the **hand**: to break a hand: One pupil broke his hand.
die Hauptschule, -n	the intermediate school
herum/reißen (i, i): Sie riß das Steuer herum.	to **tear around**: She tore the wheel around.
hin/kriegen: Das kriegen wir noch hin. (= Das Problem lösen wir noch.)	to **get**: We'll get that yet. (= We'll solve that problem yet.)
die Hoffnung, -en	the hope
kritisch	critical, critically
das Kühlwasser	the cooling water
die Kupplung (→ kuppeln)	the clutch
das Kupplungspedal, -e	the clutch pedal
Land und Leute: Wir wollen hier Land und Leute kennenlernen.	**the country and the people**: We want to get to know the country and the people.
laufen lassen A: Der Fahrer läßt den Motor laufen.	to **leave running**: The driver leaves the motor running.
das **Lebensjahr**, -e: Er hat das 7. Lebensjahr erreicht.	the **year of life**: He has reached his seventh year.
leicht haben: Sie haben es leicht mit dem automatischen Getriebe.	to **have s. th. easy**: You (they) have it easy with the automatic shift.

lenken A: Kannst du ein Auto lenken?
das **Lernziel, -e:** Er hat das Lernziel erreicht.
leuchten: ein leuchtendes Beispiel
los sein: Was war hier gestern los?

los/fahren (= ab/fahren)
los/lassen A (er läßt los, ie, a): Lassen Sie jetzt die Kupplung los!
die Luft (hier: der Luftdruck)
die Mauer, -n
der Mitschüler, —
der Mut
mutig
nach/schauen: Ich schaue mal in meinem Buch nach.
naturwissenschaftlich: ein naturwissenschaftlich ausgerichtetes Gymnasium
der **Nerv, -en:** die Nerven behalten: Christa hat die Nerven behalten.
neusprachlich: ein neusprachliches Gymnasium

das Öl (im Motor)
die Orientierungsstufe, -n

die Panik: voller Panik
die Parklücke, -n
qualifizieren: ein qualifizierender Abschluß (an der Schule)
die Realschule, -n
recht: So ist es recht!
rechts: rechts ran fahren
die **Rede, -n:** eine Rede halten: Er hielt eine Rede.
die Reife (an der Schule)
rein: Jetzt den 1. Gang rein!
ins **Rollen** kommen: Der Wagen kam auf der abschüssigen Straße ins Rollen.
der Ruck: mit einem harten Ruck
der Rückspiegel, —
der Rückwärtsgang, ⸗e
sagen: Wer sagt's denn! (= Wer hat denn gesagt, daß das zu schwierig ist?)
schaffen: Sie schaffen das noch. (= Sie lernen das noch.)
schmal: eine schmale Straße
schön (hier: richtig)
das Schuljahr, -e
die Schulpflicht

to **steer:** Can you steer a car?
the **education goal:** He has reached his educational goal.
to shine: a shining example
to **be happening:** What was going on here yesterday?

to drive away, to drive off
to **let go, to release:** Now release the clutch.
the air (here: the air pressure)
the wall
the schoolmate
the courage
courageous
to **look and see:** I'll check in my book.

of the natural sciences: a preparatory high school emphasizing the natural sciences
the **nerve:** to keep one's nerves: Christa kept her nerves.
of modern languages: a preparatory high school emphasizing the modern languages

the oil (in the motor)
the placement and orientation class (for transfer to a higher-level school)

the panic: complete panic
the parking space
to qualify: a certificate (or diploma) of qualification
the intermediate high school
correct: That's the right way!
(to, on) the right: Pull up on the right.
the **speech:** to hold a speech: He held a speech.
the certificate, the diploma
into: Now into first gear!
to **start to roll:** The car started to roll on the steep street.
the jolt: with a hard jolt
the rear-view mirror
the reverse gear
to **say:** Who says that? (= Who said that that is too difficult?)
to **make, to do:** You'll do it yet. (You'll learn that yet.)
narrow: a narrow street
nicely (here: correctly)
the school year
the mandatory education

schulpflichtig	required to attend school, of school age
der Schultyp, -en	the type of school
schwimmen (a, o)	to swim
die Schwimmstunde, -n	the swimming class
sehen: Na, sehen Sie! (hier: Ich habe es gleich gesagt/gedacht.)	to **see**: There, you see! (I (already) told you so.)
die Situation, -en	the situation
sogenannt	so-called
stehen: zum Stehen kommen: Der Wagen kam an der Mauer zum Stehen.	to **stand**: to come to a standstill: The car came to a standstill at the wall.
das Steuer, —	the steering wheel
stoppen = an/halten	to stop = to halt
strahlen: mit strahlendem Lächeln	to beam: with a beaming smile
die Straßenverkehrsordnung	the traffic regulations
die Stunde, -n (hier: die Unterrichtsstunde)	the hour, the class (here: the class instruction)
tanken	to refuel, to fill up
die Tankstelle, -n	the gas station
der Tankwart, -e	the gas station attendant
die Tat, -en	the deed
die Teilzeit-Pflichtschule, -n (= eine Schule, die nicht jeden Tag besucht wird)	the part-time mandatory school (= a school which is not attended every day)
toll sein: Das war toll!	to **be fantastic**: That was fantastic!
treten (er tritt, a, e): Ich trete jetzt das Pedal.	to **step**: Now I'm stepping on the pedal.
der Übergang: der Übergang in die Realschule	the transition, the transfer: the transfer to intermediate high school
übergeben (er übergibt, a, e): Man übergab ihr die Urkunde.	to **present**: The certificate was presented to her.
überhaupt nicht = gar nicht	not at all
über/wechseln: Er will ins Gymnasium überwechseln.	to **transfer**: He wants to transfer to the preparatory high school.
üblich: wie üblich (= wie immer)	usual: as usual (= as always)
der Umstand, ̈e: unter Umständen (u. U.)	the circumstance: under certain circumstances
uneigennützig	unselfish
das Unheil	the disaster
der Unfall, ̈e	the accident
das Universitätsstudium	the study at a university, the college and graduate school education
unverletzt	uninjured
das Verhalten	the behavior
verhüten A: Sie hat durch ihre Tat ein Unheil verhütet.	to **prevent**: Through her deed she prevented a disaster.
der Verleihungsausschuß, ̈(ss)e (für Orden, Medaillen usw.)	the awards committee (for orders, medals, etc.)
die Verletzung, -en: eine schwere Verletzung	the injury: a serious injury
verlieren A (o, o): den Mut verlieren: Verlieren Sie nicht den Mut!	to **lose**: to lose courage: Don't lose courage!

versammelt sein: Alle Schüler waren vor der Schule versammelt.
to be gathered: All the pupils were gathered in front of the school.

die Verwaltung, -en
the administration

die Verzweiflungstat, -en
the act of desperation

vorbildlich
exemplary

der Vorfall, ⸚e = das Ereignis, -se
the occurrence, the event

wahrscheinlich
probable, probably

warm halten: Er hält den Raum warm.
to keep warm: He is keeping the room warm.

wechseln: Er hat die Schule gewechselt.
to change: He changed schools.

weg sein: Der Wagen steht ein bißchen weit von der Bordsteinkante weg.
to be away: The car is a bit far away from the curb.

die Windschutzscheibe, -n
the windshield

wirtschaftswissenschaftlich: ein wirtschaftswissenschaftlich ausgerichtetes Gymnasium
of the economic sciences: a (limited) preparatory high school specializing in economics and business

der Zeitungsausschnitt, -e
the newspaper clipping

zersplittern: die zersplitterte Scheibe
to smash: the smashed windshield

der Zugang: den Zugang eröffnen: Das Zeugnis eröffnet den Zugang zur öffentlichen Verwaltung.
the access: to provide access: The certificate provides access to public administration.

zurück/legen: Wir haben mit unserem Wagen an einem Tag 900 Kilometer zurückgelegt.
to place behind: We've covered 900 kilometers in our car on one day.

zu/schreiben A + D (ie, ie): Er schrieb die Rettung dem mutigen Verhalten des Mädchens zu.
to attribute to: He attributed the rescue to the girl's courageous behavior.

zusammen/fassen: Die neuen Schüler werden in einer Klasse zusammengefaßt.
to summarize, to bring together: The new pupils are brought together in one class.

sich zu/ziehen (o, o): Sie hat sich bei dem Unfall Verletzungen zugezogen.
to incur: She incurred injuries in the accident.

der Zweifel, —: Es gibt keinen Zweifel.
the doubt: There is no doubt.

zweifellos
without doubt

Abschnitt 5

das Abdeckmaterial, -materialien (→ ab/decken A): Material, das zum Abdecken von Maschinen usw. gebraucht wird.
the protective covering: Material, which is used for the protective covering of machines, etc.

der Abfall, ⸚e
the trash

ab/geben A (er gibt ab, a, e): Geben Sie die Schlüssel bitte bei mir ab.
to hand in, or over: Please leave your keys with me.

die Abholung (→ ab/holen A): Heute wird der Müll abgeholt.
the collection: The rubbish is being collected today.

die Ablagerung, -en: die Ablagerung von Müll, von alten Autoreifen
the deposit, the dumping: the dumping of garbage, of old tires

ab/marschieren: Wann marschieren wir morgen von hier ab?
to march off: When are we going to march off from here tomorrow?

ab/melden A: Ich habe mein Auto bei der Polizei abgemeldet.

ab/stellen A: Dort hat jemand sein Auto abgestellt.

ab/transportieren A: Morgen früh wird der Müll abtransportiert.

die Aktion, -en

alkoholfrei (= ohne Alkohol): alkoholfreie Getränke

alle: Der Müll wird alle 14 Tage abgeholt.

allerdings: Ich komme mit euch mit. Allerdings muß ich bis um 6 Uhr wieder zu Hause sein.

an/kommen lassen auf: Wir wollen es nicht darauf ankommen lassen, daß uns die Polizei erwischt.

an/nehmen A (er nimmt an, a, o): Nehmen Sie auch US-Dollars an?

die Arbeitskolonne, -n (= eine Gruppe von Arbeitern, die für eine bestimmte Arbei abgestellt worden ist)

auf/machen A (hier: trinken): Wollen wir uns jetzt eine Flasche Wein aufmachen?

aus/brennen: ein ausgebranntes Auto

aus/füllen A: Muß ich dieses Formular noch ausfüllen?

ausgerechnet: Heute wollten wir fortfahren, und ausgerechnet heute muß es regnen.

aus/rüsten A mit: Die Schüler waren bei der Aktion mit Leiterwagen und Schubkarren ausgerüstet.

der Autobesitzer, —

der Autofriedhof, ⸚e

der Autoreifen, —

das Autowrack, -s

der Bahnreisende, -n

begünstigen A: Das warme Wetter begünstigt den Fremdenverkehr.

bereits: Wir waren in diesem Jahr bereits zweimal in Paris.

beseitigen A: Wer beseitigt den Müll? Macht das die Gemeinde oder eine Privatfirma?

die Besprechung, -en

bestens (= sehr gut)

der Beweis, -e

die Bierdose, -n

die Bierflasche, -n

to **cancel:** I cancelled the registration of my car with the police.

to **put away, to park:** Somebody parked his car there.

to **cart away:** The rubbish will be carted away tomorrow.

the action

non-alcoholic (= without alcohol): non-alcoholic beverages

all, every: The garbage is collected every 14 days.

however: I'm coming with you. However, I have to be home again by 6 o'clock.

to **let (s. th.) depend upon:** We don't want to take the risk of the police catching us.

to **accept:** Do you accept U.S. dollars?

the work column, the work team (= a group of workers, which has been selected to do a certain job)

to **open** (here: to drink): Shall we open a bottle of wine now?

to burn out: a burned out car

to **fill out:** Do I still have to fill out this form?

just, exactly: We wanted to leave today, and today, of all days, it has to rain.

to **equip:** The pupils were equipped for the project with rack-wagons and push-carts.

the automobile owner

the car cemetery

the car tire

the car wreck

the train passenger

to **encourage:** The warm weather encourages tourism.

already: We were already in Paris twice this year.

to **remove:** Who removes the garbage? Does the municipal government do it, or a private company?

the conference

fine, well (= very good, very well)

the proof

the beer can

the beer bottle

das Bußgeld, -er (= die Polizeistrafe, -n) — the penalty (= the fine imposed by police)
der Bußgeldkatalog, -e — the regulations regarding fines
da sein: Ich bin gleich wieder da. (= bei dir/euch/Ihnen) — to be there: I'll be right back. (with you, at your place)
dergleichen: und dergleichen (u. dgl.) — and such, and similar things
die Einführung (= ein/führen A: Ein neuer Bußgeldkatalog wurde eingeführt.) — the introduction: A new set of regulations on fines was introduced.
ein/packen A: Soll ich Ihnen die Sachen einpacken? — to pack: Shall I pack your things?
einzeln: einzelne Klassen, einzelne Leute — individual: individual classes, individual people

entlang: entlang der Bahnlinie — along: along the railroad
entwerten A: der entwertete Fahrschein — to cancel: the cancelled ticket
erfassen A (= verstehen A): Die Leute haben den Zweck des Umweltschutzes noch nicht erfaßt. — to grasp, to understand: People still haven't understood the purpose of environmental protection.
erfolgen: Die Handlung (= Aktion) erfolgt zugunsten einer Person. — to take place: The action takes place for the benefit of one person.
erfreulich: Es ist erfreulich, daß ... — gratifying: It is gratifying, that ...
das Ergebnis, -se (= das Resultat, -e) — the outcome (the result)
erheben A (o, o): Wieviel Bußgeld wird für falsches Parken erhoben? — to impose: How much of a fine is imposed for incorrect parking?
erheblich (= bedeutend) — significant(ly)
erledigen A: Fräulein Schmidt muß noch die heutige Post erledigen. — to take care of: Miss Schmidt still has to take care of today's mail.
der Fachlehrer, — — the teacher of a special subject
der Fahrschüler, — (= ein Schüler, der regelmäßig mit dem Bus oder mit der Bahn zur Schule fährt) — the commuter (= a pupil who regularly travels to school by train or bus)
der Fahrzeughalter, — — the motor vehicle owner
feiern A: Heute feiern wir unseren Hochzeitstag. — to celebrate: We're celebrating our wedding anniversary today.
fein: Das ist fein (= schön). — fine: That is fine (= nice).
der Fernseher, — (= der Fernsehapparat) — the television set
fest/stellen — to establish, to find out
die Flur, -en: Wald und Flur — the field: woods and fields
fort/werfen A (er wirft fort, a, o): Wer hat die leere Zigarettenschachtel fortgeworfen? — to throw away: Who threw away the empty cigarette package?
früher oder später: Früher oder später wird alles einmal fortgeworfen. — sooner or later: Sooner or later everything will be thrown away.
das Frühlingswetter — the spring weather
die Fußballübertragung, -en (im Radio oder Fernsehen) — the soccer broadcast (on radio or television)
gefräßig: ein gefräßiges Tier — voracious: a voracious animal
die Gemeinde, -n: die Gemeinde Ainring — the municipality: the municipality of Ainring
das Gemeindegebiet, -e — the municipal area
gemütlich: Wir sitzen hier so gemütlich zusammen. — pleasant(ly): We're enjoying each other's company so much.

geringer (= weniger)
das Geschenkpapier (= Papier zum Verpacken von Geschenken)
das Getränk, -e
die Getränkedose, -n
gleich: Bis gleich!

gleichzeitig = zu gleicher Zeit; zur gleichen Zeit
glotzen (in den Fernseher): fern/sehen, Fernsehen schauen
der Grund, "-e: aus diesem Grunde
sich **handeln** um A: Worum handelte es sich bei dem Gespräch?
die **Handlung, -en** (= die Aktion, -en): In dem Satz „Peter arbeitet" drückt das Verb ‚arbeiten' eine Handlung aus. In dem Satz „Der Motor arbeitet" drückt das Verb ‚arbeiten' einen Vorgang aus.
hauptsächlich (= in erster Linie)
herrlich: Heute ist herrliches Wetter.

her/stellen A (= produzieren): Wer stellt diese Maschinen her?
der Hochzeitstag, -e
ideal
illegal
der Inhalt, -e (= die Bedeutung, -en)

inhaltsleer (= ohne Inhalt/Bedeutung)

inhaltslos: In Verbindung mit bestimmten Verben steht das Pronomen *es* als inhaltsloses Subjekt.
der Karton, -s
die Käseschachtel, -n
der Kfz-Brief, -e (= Kraftfahrzeug-Brief) = die amtliche Besitzurkunde über ein Kraftfahrzeug
die Kleider (Plural)
kommen: Das alte Verpackungsmaterial kommt in die Mülltonne.
kostenlos
der Kühlschrank, "-e
sich **kümmern** um A: Wir müssen uns jetzt um unsere Gäste kümmern.
lachen: Wir haben hier nichts zu lachen. (Uns geht es hier nicht gut.)

die Landschaft, -en

less
the gift wrap (= paper for the wrapping of presents)
the drink
the can (for drinks)
right away, immediately: See you in a moment!

simultaneously = at the same time

to stare (at the television set) = to watch television
the reason: for this reason
to **be a matter of:** What was the discussion about?
the **action:** In the sentence "Peter works", the verb 'to work' expresses an action. In the sentence "The motor works", the verb 'to work' expresses an occurrence.
main(ly) (= primarily)
marvelous: The weather is marvelous today.

to **manufacture** (= to produce): Who manufactures these machines?
the wedding day, the wedding anniversary
ideal
illegal
the content, the meaning (= the significance)
insubstantial (= without meaning/significance)

insignificant: The pronoun *es* stands in combination with certain verbs as a "false" subject.
the carton
the cheese package
the motor vehicle registration = the official document of ownership of a motor vehicle
the clothes
to **come:** The old packaging material lands in the garbage can.
free of charge
the refrigerator
to **take care of:** We have to attend to our guests now.
to **laugh:** There's absolutely nothing to laugh about here. (Our situation is prety serious at the moment.
the countryside, the landscape

landen: Die alten Briefe landen einmal
alle in der Mülltonne.

sich **langweilen:** Ich habe mich den ganzen Tag gelangweilt.

die Lavendelseife, -n
der Leiterwagen
der Liebesbrief, -e

los/werden: Wo kann man hier die Abfäl-
le loswerden?

die Menge, -n
der **Mitmensch, -en:** Zu seinen Mitmen-
schen soll man immer freundlich sein.

die Müllabfuhr (= den Müll ab/fahren)
die Müllhalde, -n
der Müllsack, ⁻e
die Mülltonne, -n
der Müllwagen, —
der Nagelstock, ⁻e (= ein Stock mit einem
Nagel an einem Ende, mit dem man auf
dem Boden liegendes Papier aufspießt)

nahezu (= fast): Als wir heimkamen, war
es nahezu Mitternacht.

das Neubaugebiet, -e
die Öffnung, -en

organisieren: Hier ist die Müllabfuhr bestens organisiert.

originell: auf originelle Weise
die Packung, -en

passen: Der Abfall paßt nicht mehr in unsere Mülltonne.

die Plastiktüte, -n
die Polizeidienststelle, -n
das Produkt, -e

prall: Die Müllsäcke sind prall gefüllt.

die Rechnung, -en
der Reifen (→ der Autoreifen, —)

reinigen A: Die Straßen werden täglich ge-
reinigt.

rüber/kommen (er kommt rüber, a, o):
(umgangssprachlich für: hinüber/kom-
men): Warte! Ich komm rüber!

die Satzeinleitung, -en

die Säuberungsaktion, -en
das Schrottauto, -s (= ein Auto, das ver-
schrottet werden soll)
der Schrottplatz, ⁻e
die Schubkarre, -n
das Schulhaus, ⁻er

---

to **land:** Sometime or other the old letters
all land in the garbage can.

to **be bored:** I was bored the whole day.

the lavender soap
the rack-wagon
the love letter

to **dispose of:** Where can trash be disposed
of here?

the quantity
the **fellow human being:** People should always be friendly to one another.

the refuse removal
the garbage dump
the rubbish bag
the garbage can
the garbage truck
the scrap picker (= a rod with a nail at one
end for picking up pieces of paper lying
around on the ground)

nearly (= almost): It was almost midnight
when we came home.

the area of new housing developments
the opening

to **organize:** The garbage removal is orga-
nized very well here.

original(ly): in an original manner
the package

to **fit:** The trash doesn't fit into our garbage can anymore.

the plastic bag
the police precinct
the product

tight(ly): The rubbish bags are filled tight-
ly.

the bill
the tire (the car tire)
to **clean:** The streets are cleaned every day.

to **come over:** (everyday language for: to
come over): Wait! I'm coming over.

the beginning of the sentence, the sentence
introduction
the clean-up project
the scrap car (= a car, which is going to be
scrapped)
the scrap dumping ground
the pushcart
the schoolhouse

schütten A: Schütten Sie den Abfall in die Mülltonne!

to **empty**: Empty the trash into the garbage can!

schön: Es ist schön, daß du mich heute anrufst.

nice: It's nice that you called me today.

die Seife, -n

the soap

sein: Bist du's? — Ja, ich bin's.

to **be**: Is that you? — Yes, it's me.

so = auf diese Weise

thus = in this manner

sowie = ebenso

just as, just like

der Sperrmüll

the bulk refuse

städtisch: die städtische Müllabfuhr

urban: the urban refuse removal

die Strafe, -n

the penalty

das Stück, -e

the piece

teilweise

partial(ly)

teuer kommen D: Der Umweltschutz kommt uns teuer.

to **be costly**: Environmental protection is costly.

der Trick, -s

the trick

der Umweltschutz

the environmental protection

der Umweltverschmutzer, — (= jemand, der die Umwelt verschmutzt)

the polluter (= someone who pollutes the environment)

unerlaubt = verboten

not allowed = forbidden, prohibited

der Unrat

the refuse

der **Verdacht**: Der Verdacht liegt nahe, daß ...

the **suspicion**: It might well be suspected that ...

verdeutlichen = deutlich machen A

to clarify = to make clear

verlieren (o, o): Ich habe meinen Geldbeutel verloren.

to **lose**: I lost my change purse.

die Verpackung, -en

the packaging

die Verpackungsindustrie, -n

the packaging industry

das Verpackungsmaterial, -materialien

the packaging material

die Verschönerung (→ verschönern A): die Verschönerung der Landschaft

the beautification: the beautification of the countryside

verschwinden (a, u): Der Unrat ist von der Straße verschwunden.

to **disappear**: The refuse has disappeared from the street.

verstreuen A: Der Wind hat das Papier über die Straße verstreut.

to **scatter**: The wind scattered the paper all over the street.

die Verzichtserklärung, -en (= eine Mitteilung, daß man auf etwas verzichten will)

the declaration of renunciation (= a statement that one wants to renounce something)

das Waldstück, -e

the part of the woods

der Waldweg, -e

the path in the woods

der Wandertag, -e

the excursion

der Wanderweg, -e

the path for hiking or walking

die Wegstrecke, -n

the distance, the stretch of road, or path

weg/werfen A (er wirft weg, a, o): Werfen Sie die alten Zeitungen weg!

to **throw away**: Throw away the old newspapers!

die Weinflasche, -n

the wine bottle

die Zahnpasta

the toothpaste

ziehen (o, o): Die Schüler ziehen mit ihren Lehrern durch die schöne Landschaft.

to **move**: The students walk with their teachers through the lovely countryside.

die Zigarettenpackung, -en	the cigarette package
die Zigarettenschachtel, -n	the cigarette pack, or box
die Zivilisationsreste (Plural): (figurativ: die Dinge, die weggeworfen werden)	the remains of civilization: (figurative: objects which are thrown away)
zugunsten = für	for the benefit of = for
die Zulassungsstelle (für Kraftfahrzeuge)	the registration office (for motor vehicles)
zurück/lassen A (er läßt zurück, ie, a): Die Leute haben die Müllsäcke zur Abholung durch die Gemeinde am Weg zurückgelassen.	to **leave behind**: The people left the rubbish bags behind on the path for collection by the municipality.
zurück/legen: Heute haben wir einen weiten Weg zurückgelegt.	to **put behind, to cover**: We covered a lot of territory today.
zusammen/sitzen (a, e): Wir wollen ein bißchen gemütlich zusammensitzen.	to **sit around together**: We want to sit around and enjoy each other's company.
zu/teilen D + A: Jede Schulklasse hat ein bestimmtes Gebiet zugeteilt bekommen.	to **assign**: Each school class had a specific area assigned to it.
der Zweck, -e: der Zweck des Umweltschutzes	the purpose: the purpose of environmental protection

Abschnitt 6

ab/brechen A (er bricht ab, a, o): Der Pilot hat seinen Übungsflug abgebrochen.	to **discontinue**: The pilot discontinued his practice flight.
ab/hauen (umgangssprachlich für weg/gehen): Hau ab!	to **scram** (everyday language for: to leave): Get lost!
ab/nehmen A (er nimmt ab, a, o): Er nimmt seinen Helm ab.	to **take off, to remove**: He takes off his helmet.
ab/schalten A: Er hat die Maschine abgeschaltet.	to **stop, to turn off**: He stopped the machine engine.
ab/statten A: Wir wollen unserem Chef einen Besuch abstatten.	to **pay** (a visit): We want to pay a visit to our director.
ab/stellen A: Können Sie das Geräusch in dem Radioapparat abstellen?	to **remove**: Can you eliminate the noise in the radio?
die Abteilung, -en (im Krankenhaus)	the ward (in a hospital)
ab/wenden A: Wir können die Gefahr nicht abwenden.	to **avert**: We can't avert the danger.
die **Ahnung, -en**: Du hast vielleicht eine Ahnung! (= Du weißt ja überhaupt nichts.)	the **notion**: You don't have the faintest idea! (= You have no idea what's going on.)
alarmieren A: Wer hat die Feuerwehr alarmiert?	to **alarm, to notify**: Who called the fire department?
ander-: unter anderem (u. a.)	other: among other things
an/geben A (er gibt an, a, e): Können Sie mir die Zahl der Verletzten angeben?	to **state, to indicate**: Can you tell me how many persons have been injured?
an/gehören D: Mein Kollege gehört dem Betriebsrat an.	to **belong to**: My colleague belongs to the council of employees' representatives.
angeln	to fish

der Arbeitnehmer, —
the employee

der Arbeitskollege, -n
the colleague

der Atem: außer Atem
the breath: out of breath

die Atemspende (bei einem Bewußtlosen)
the artificial respiration (in the case of an unconscious person)

atmen: Der Verletzte atmet nur sehr schwach.
to **breathe:** The injured person ist breathing very weakly.

die Atmung
the breathing

der Aufklärungsflug, ⁻e
the reconnaissance flight

das Aufklärungsgeschwader, —
the reconnaissance squadron

sich **auf/setzen** A: Der Pilot setzte sich seinen Helm auf.
to **put on:** The pilot put on his helmet.

der Auftrag, ⁻e
the assignment, the order

die Ausatmung (→ aus/atmen)
the exhalation

aus/geben A (er gibt aus, a, e): Mein Kollege gibt einen aus. (= Er zahlt für uns alle ein Bier/einen Schnaps. = Er lädt uns zu einem Glas Bier/Schnaps ein.)
to **give out, to pay:** The drinks are on my colleague. (= He's paying for a round of beer/schnaps. = He's inviting us to a glass of beer/schnaps.)

aus/setzen: Der Motor hat ausgesetzt.
to **stop suddenly:** The motor stopped suddenly.

bandagieren: Dem Verletzten wurde das gebrochene Bein bandagiert.
to **bandage:** The broken leg of the injured person was bandaged.

die Bank, -en
the bank

die Beatmung (→ beatmen)
the respiration

sich **beeilen:** Ich beeile mich.
to **hurry:** I'm hurrying.

sich **befinden:** Wo befindet sich hier die nächste Polizeidienststelle?
to **be** (located): Where is the nearest police station?

begrenzen A: Das „Satzfeld" wird von den Prädikatsteilen begrenzt.
to **circumscribe:** The sentence field is surrounded by the parts of the verb.

beheben: Man will die Unfallfolgen beheben.
to **eliminate, to reduce:** One wants to reduce the immediate dangers.

behindert: Die Atmung des Verletzten war behindert.
to **impede:** The breathing of the injured person was impeded.

bei/tragen (er trägt bei, u, a): Wir tragen auch unseren Teil dazu bei, daß nicht so viele Unfälle passieren.
to **contribute:** We're contributing our share to the prevention of accidents.

die Belegschaft, -en
the personnel, the staff, the emplyees

bemerken: Der Pilot bemerkte in seiner Maschine ein Geräusch.
to **notice:** The pilot noticed a noise in his airplane.

die Bemühung, -en (→ sich bemühen um)
the effort

beobachten A: Haben Sie auch den Übungsflug beobachtet?
to **observe:** Did you also observe the practice flight?

der Beruf, -e
the profession, the job

beruflich: Ich bin beruflich in dieser Stadt.
on **business:** I'm in this city on business.

sich **beschäftigen mit:** Ich beschäftige mich schon seit längerer Zeit mit sozialen Fragen.
to **occupy oneself with:** I've been concerned with social questions for a long time already.

Bescheid sagen (informieren): Sagen Sie bitte meiner Frau Bescheid, daß ich heute später komme.
to **inform, to let know:** Please let my wife know that I'll be home late today.

besteigen (ie, ie): Der Pilot bestieg seine Maschine.

to climb into: The pilot climbed into his airplane.

der Betrieb, -e

the factory, the firm, the business, the company

die Betriebsleitung, -en

the management

der Betriebsrat, "̈e

the council of employees' representatives

beugen: Beugen Sie dem Verletzten den Kopf nach hinten.

to bend, to lean: Lean the head of the injured person back.

bewahren: Bitte Ruhe bewahren!

to keep: Please keep calm!

bewußtlos: der Bewußtlose, -n

unconscious: the unconscious person

die Bewußtlosigkeit

the unconsciousness

der Brand, "̈e

the fire

breit lachen: Bert lachte breit und sagte, ...

to laugh heartily: Bert laughed heartily and said, ...

der Bruch, "̈e (z. B. der Beinbruch)

the fracture (for example, the leg fracture)

bzw. = beziehungsweise

respectively, that is

der Daumen, —

the thumb

daraufhin = danach

thereupon

die Decke, -n (z. B. die Bettdecke, -n)

the cover (for example, the bed spread)

dicht: ziemlich dichter Verkehr

dense, heavy: quite heavy traffic

dröhnen: Der Flugzeugmotor dröhnt.

to rumble, to drone: The plane engine rumbles.

eigentlich

actual(ly), real(ly)

es eilig haben: Warum haben Sie es so eilig?

to be in a hurry: Why are you in such a hurry?

ein/blasen (z. B. Luft)

to breathe into, to blow into (for example, air)

der Eingang, "̈e

the entrance

ein/hängen A: Ich habe sofort den Telefonhörer eingehängt.

to hang up: I hung up (the telephone receiver) immediately.

ein/setzen: Nach kurzer Zeit setzte bei dem Verletzten die Atmung wieder ein.

to start, to begin: After a short time the injured person began breathing.

die Einstellung, -en (→ ein/stellen A): die Einstellung von Personal

the hiring: the hiring of personnel

ein/treffen (er trifft ein, a, o): Die Feuerwehr ist in kurzer Zeit eingetroffen.

to arrive: The firemen arrived quickly.

das Ende: am Ende der Stadt; am anderen Ende der Leitung

the end: at the end of the city; at the other end of the line

entdecken A: In der Nacht entdeckte er im Zelt eine Maus.

to discover: During the night he discovered a mouse in his tent.

enttäuscht sein: Er war über den geringen Erfolg enttäuscht.

to be disappointed: He was disappointed about the minimal success.

das Ereignis, -se

the event

erhalten A (er erhält, ie, a): Wir müssen die vertrauensvolle Zusammenarbeit weiterhin erhalten.

to maintain: We have to further maintain the cooperation based on mutual confidence and trust.

der Erlaubnisschein, -e: (Hier: eine Bescheinigung, die einem Arbeitnehmer erlaubt, die Fabrik während der Arbeitszeit zu verlassen)

the permit: (here: a form which permits an employee to leave the factory during work hours)

die Erste-Hilfe-Leistung → Erste-Hilfe leisten — the first aid

erwähnen A: Er hat nichts von der Angelegenheit erwähnt. — to **mention**: He mentioned nothing about the matter.

erwidern (= antworten) — to reply (= to answer)

es: Es ist da. (= Das Kind ist geboren.) — it: It has arrived. (= The child has been born.)

der Facharbeiter, — — the skilled worker

der Fall, ⁺e: für alle Fälle (= vorsorglich) — the case: inany case (= just in case)

feiern A: Er feiert seinen Geburtstag. — to **celebrate**: He is celebrating his birthday.

die Festlegung → fest/legen A: Die Arbeitszeit wird neu festgelegt. — the regulation: The work hours are being rescheduled.

die Feuerwehr, -en — the firemen, the fire department

der Feuerwehrmann, ⁺er oder -leute — the fireman

der Fliegerhelm, -e — the flight helmet

die Fliegerkombination, -en — the flight suit

fluchen — to curse

das Flugfeld, -er — the airfield

die **Flugstunde, -n**: Wir waren zwei Flugstunden unterwegs. — the **flight hour**: We were in the air for two flight hours.

der Flugzeugführer, — — the pilot

fort/setzen: Er setzt seine Arbeit fort. — to **continue**: He continues his work.

die Frage, -n: eine soziale Frage — the question: a social question

der Funk: über Funk — the wireless: on the wireless

der Gang, ⁺e = der Korridor, -e — the hallway = the corridor

die Gefahr, -en — the danger

gegenüber: mein Gegenüber = mein Gesprächspartner — opposite: my opposite = my conversation partner

gehen: Das geht in Ordnung. = Das ist in Ordnung. — to **go**: That's in order. = That's o. k.

das Geräusch, -e — the noise

das Gesicht, -er — the face

das Gestell, -e — the rack

die Gewalt: ohne Gewalt = vorsichtig — the force: without force = carefully, gently

das Gewerkschaftsmitglied, -er — the union member

die Glasscheibe, -n: hinter der Glasscheibe = hinter dem Schalterfenster — the glass pane: behind the glass pane = behind the counter window

glauben an A: Der Polizist glaubte an einen Mordfall. = Er vermutete einen Mordfall. — to **believe** (in): The policeman believed it to be a murder. (= He suspected a murder.)

gratulieren D zu: Ich gratuliere dir zum Geburtstag. — to **congratulate** s. o. on: I congratulate you on your birthday.

die Grundregel, -n — the fundamental rule

der Grundsatz, ⁺e — the principle

gut: eine gute Stunde nach der Mittagspause — good: a good hour after the lunch break

der Hauptfeldwebel, — — the master sergeant

heftig: durch heftiges Klopfen — vigorous(ly): by vigorous knocking

der Helm, -e (hier: der Fliegerhelm, -e) — the helmet (here: the flight helmet)

heraus/ragen: Aus dem Kofferraum ragte ein Arm heraus.

to protrude: An arm protruded from the trunk.

heraus/stellen: Später stellte sich heraus, daß ...

to turn out: Later it turned out that ...

herein/rufen A (ie, u): Der Arzt rief mich herein.

to call in: The doctor called me in.

herrschen: Es herrschte eine Mäuseplage.

to dominate, to be: There was a mouse plague.

die Hilfe, -n

the aid, the help

Hilfe leisten D: Die Passanten leisteten dem Verletzten Hilfe.

to give aid: The passers-by helped the injured person.

Hilfe: zu Hilfe rufen: Der Verletzte rief die Passanten zu Hilfe.

help: to call for help: The injured person called to the passers-by for help.

huschen: Plötzlich huschte eine Maus durch das Zelt.

to flit: Suddenly a mouse flitted through the tent.

die Informationssäule, -n

the information post

sich **informieren** über A: Ich habe mich genau über die Aufgaben des Betriebsrats informiert.

to inform o. s. about: I've informed myself exactly about the tasks and duties of the employees' council.

insgesamt = zusammen

altogether

irritieren: Das Geräusch irritierte den Piloten.

to irritate: The noise irritated the pilot.

jedoch = aber

however = but

der Junge, -n (Gegensatz: das Mädchen, —)

the boy (opposite: the girl)

die Kantine, -n

the canteen

die Karriere, -n (im Beruf)

the career (in professional life)

die Kasse (= der Kassenschalter in einer Bank)

the cash register, the cashier (= the cashier's window in a bank)

keuchen: Noch ganz außer Atem keuchte Bert ins Telefon ...

to gasp: Still completely out of breath, Bert gasped into the phone ...

das Kinn

the chin

klären A: Wir wollen einige Fragen klären.

to clarify: We want to clarify a few questions.

das Kleidungsstück, -e

the piece of clothing

klettern: Er kletterte durch das Fenster.

to climb: He climbed through the window.

klopfen: Er klopfte mit der Hand gegen seinen Helm. — Er klopfte an die Tür.

to knock: He knocked on his helmet with his hand. — He knocked on the door.

die Kneipe, -n

the bar, the pub

der Kofferraum, ⁻e (im Auto)

the trunk (in a car)

der Kollege, -n

the colleague

der Kopf, ⁻e: von Kopf bis Fuß (= von oben bis unten = vollkommen)

the head: from head to toe (= from top to bottom = completely)

das Krankenhaus, ⁻er

the hospital

die Krankenkasse, -n = die Krankenversicherung, -en

the health insurance

der Krankenwagen, —

the ambulance

das Kreuz, -e: ein rotes Kreuz; das Rote Kreuz

the cross: a red cross; the Red Cross

kriegen = bekommen

to get, to receive

der Kunde, -n

the client, the customer

die Kündigung, -en (von Personal)	the dismissal (of personnel)
der Kurs, -e (z. B. der D-Mark-Kurs, der Dollar-Kurs)	the exchange rate (for example, the exchange rate for German marks, the exchange rate for dollars)
die Landung, -en	the landing
lebensbedrohend: eine lebensbedrohende Krankheit	fatal: a fatal disease
die **Lebensgefahr**: Vorsicht Lebensgefahr!	the **danger** (to life): Caution — Danger!
die Leiche, -n	the corpse
die Leiter, -n	the ladder
die Leitung, -en (= die Telefonleitung, -en)	the wire, the line (= the telephone line)
los/gehen: Es geht los. (hier: Er fährt los.)	to **start, to begin, to leave**: It's starting. (here: He's departing.)
die Luft: Luft holen = ein/atmen	the air: to breathe deeply = to inhale
der Luftweg, -e (im Körper)	the respiratory tract (in the body)
machen: Ich mache das schon. (= Ich erledige das.)	to **make, to do**: I'll do that, don't worry. (= I'll take care of that.)
manövermäßig: wie bei einem Manöver	ready for maneuver: like in a maneuver
die Maschinenhalle, -n	the machine area
die Maus, ⸚e	the mouse
die Mäuseplage, -n	the plague of mice
meinetwegen! (= Von mir aus! Ich habe nichts dagegen.)	For all I care! (= I have nothing against it.)
der Meister, —	the foreman
merkwürdig = komisch	unusual = strange
mit/bestimmen: Der Betriebsrat bestimmt bei vielen Fragen im Betrieb mit.	to **co-determine**: The council of employees' representatives exercises co-determination with regard to many company issues.
die Mittagspause, -n	the lunch break
die Möglichkeit, -en: nach Möglichkeit = möglichst	the possibility: if possible
der Mordfall, ⸚e	the murder, the case of murder
der Mund, ⸚er	the mouth
nach/folgen: der nachfolgende Verkehr	to follow, to ensue: the ensuing traffic
nach/schauen: Ich schaue nach, ob jemand im Zimmer ist.	to **look, to check**: I'll check to see if someone's in the room.
die Nase, -n	the nose
die Notlandung, -en	the emergency landing
österreichisch	Austrian
der Polizist, -en	the policeman
der Patient, -en	the patient
die **Personalfrage**: Ob wir unseren Betrieb erweitern können, ist nicht nur eine Personalfrage.	the **question of personnel**: Whether or not we enlarge our company is not only a question of personnel.
der Pförtner, —	the guard
der Pilot, -en	the pilot
politisch	political(ly)
der Praxisraum, ⸚e (eines Arztes)	the doctor's office
der Ratschlag, ⸚e	the advice

raus/lassen A (er läßt raus, ie, a): Er läßt mich nicht raus. (= Er läßt mich nicht gehen.)	to **let out:** He won't let me out. (He won't let me go.)
das Recht, -e	the law, the right
der Reisescheck, -s	the traveler's check
rennen (a, a): Ich bin zum Telefon gerannt.	to **run:** I ran to the telephone.
die **Richtung, -en:** Er fährt in Richtung Krankenhaus.	the **direction:** He drives towards the hospital.
der **Rücken, —:** Man muß den Verletzten auf den Rücken legen.	the **back:** The injured person must be laid on his back.
ruinieren A: Jetzt hat er seinen neuen Wagen ruiniert.	to **ruin:** Now he has ruined his new car.
die Runde, -n: eine Runde Bier	the round: a round of beer
sachkundig: sachkundige Hilfe	experienced, expert: expert help
scharf bremsen	to brake hard
der Schlagbaum, ⁻e	the control gate
schräg gegenüber	diagonally across
der Schrank, ⁻e	the closet, the locker
die Schranke, -n	the gate
der Schreck: zu meinem Schrecken	the horror: to my horror
schreien (ie, ie): Er schrie über die Straße.	to **scream, to yell:** He yelled across the street.
die Schulter, -n	the shoulder
die Schwester, -n (hier: die Krankenschwester, -n)	the sister, the nurse (here: the nurse)
die **Seite, -n:** Legen Sie den Verletzten auf die Seite!	the **side:** Lay the injured person on his side!
selbständig = allein	independent(ly) = by himself
sichern A: Sichern Sie den Unfallort durch ein Warndreieck!	to **secure, to block off:** Block off the scene of the accident with a warning sign!
sonst: Ich komme morgen. Wann denn sonst?	**else:** I'm coming tomorrow. When else?
sozial: eine soziale Frage	social: a social question
das Sprechzimmer, — (eines Arztes)	the consulting room (of a doctor)
springen (a, u): Er ist aus dem fahrenden Auto gesprungen.	to **jump:** He jumped out of the moving car.
die Station, -en (im Krankenhaus)	the ward (in a hospital)
zur **Stelle** sein: Der Krankenwagen war sehr schnell zur Stelle.	to **be on the spot:** The ambulance was on the spot fast.
der Stern, -e: das Gasthaus „Zum Goldenen Stern"	the star: the inn called "The Golden Star"
die **Stimme, -n:** Er hörte Stimmen.	the **voice:** He heard voices.
stolz sein auf A: Er ist sehr stolz auf seine Aufgabe im Betriebsrat.	to **be proud of:** He is very proud of his tasks and duties on the employees' council.
die Störung, -en → stören	the interruption, the interference
strahlen: Als ihm die Kollegen gratulierten, strahlte er über das ganze Gesicht.	to **beam:** He beamed from ear to ear as his colleagues congratulated him.

die Telefonmuschel, -n	the telephone receiver
die **Treppe, -n:** Gehen Sie eine Treppe hoch, dann nach rechts! Dort ist das Büro.	the **staircase, the flight of stairs:** Go one flight up, then to the right! The office is there.
überlegen A: Er überlegte, was er jetzt tun sollte.	to **contemplate:** He contemplated what he should do now.
die Überraschung, -en: zu seiner großen Überraschung	the surprise: to his great surprise
übrig bleiben: Von meinem Taschengeld ist nichts mehr übrig geblieben.	to **remain** (left over): I've spent all of my allowance.
der Übungsflug, ̈-e	the practice flight
sich **um/ziehen** (o, o): Ich ziehe mich jetzt zur Arbeit um.	to **change clothes:** I'm getting dressed for work now.
die Unfallfolgen (Plural)	the dangers after an accident
der Unfallort, -e	the scene of the accident
untergebracht sein: Die Leute waren in Zelten untergebracht.	to **be housed, to be put up:** The people were lodged in tents.
ungehindert: Jetzt kann der Verletzte ungehindert atmen.	**unimpeded:** The injured person's breathing is now unimpeded.
der Unterkiefer, −	the lower jaw
das Unterkunftszelt, -e	the lodging tent
die Unternehmensleitung, -en	the management
unterschreiben A (ie, ie): Sie haben den Scheck noch nicht unterschrieben.	to **sign:** You still haven't signed the check.
nichts **unversucht** lassen: Er wird nichts unversucht lassen. (= Er wird auf alle Fälle versuchen, ...)	to **try everything:** He'll leave no stone unturned. (He'll try in any case ...)
die Urlaubsregelung, -en	vacation regulations
die Ursache der Störung	the cause of the interference
der **Verband, ̈-e:** Die Schwester legte dem Verletzten einen Verband an.	the **bandage:** The nurse bandaged the injured person.
vergebens: Ich habe vergebens auf meinen Kollegen gewartet. Er ist nicht gekommen.	**in vain:** I waited in vain for my colleague. He didn't come.
das **Verhalten:** das Verhalten von Passanten bei Unfällen	the **behavior:** the behavior of passersby in the case of an accident
sich **verhalten** (er verhält sich, ie, a): Wie soll man sich bei Unfällen verhalten?	to **conduct o. s.:** How should one conduct oneself in the event of an accident?
verhandeln über A: Der Betriebsrat verhandelt mit der Betriebsleitung über einige Personalfragen.	to **negotiate:** The employees' council negotiates with the management about several questions regarding personnel.
der Verkehrsunfall, ̈-e	the traffic accident
verlegen (z. B. den Weg) = sperren	to block (for example, the path)
die Verletzung, -en: innere Verletzungen	the injury: internal injuries
verschließen = schließen	to lock = to close
verständigen A: Wir haben sofort die Polizei von dem Unfall verständigt.	to **inform:** We informed the police about the accident immediately.
das **Vertrauen:** Bert besitzt das Vertrauen seiner Arbeitskollegen.	the **confidence, the trust:** Bert has the confidence of his colleagues.

vertrauensvoll: vertrauensvolle Zusammenarbeit
trusting(ly): cooperation based on mutual confidence and trust

der Verunglückte → verunglücken → das Unglück
the injured person

der Vorort, -e
the suburb

wählen A: Heute wird ein neuer Betriebsrat gewählt.
to choose, to elect: A new employees' council is being elected today.

das Warndreieck, -e
the warning sign, the danger sign

die Warnleuchte, -n
the warning light

warnen A: Wir müssen die hinter uns kommenden Autofahrer warnen.
to warn: We have to warn the drivers behind us.

die Wartezeit, -en
the waiting time

das Wartezimmer, —
the waiting room

weg/kommen (a, o): So billig kommst du uns nicht weg! (= Du mußt schon etwas mehr spendieren.)
to get away: You're not going to get away so cheaply! (=You have to be a bit more generous!)

weg/ziehen A (o, o):(hier: weg/schaffen, zur Seite schaffen)
to move away: (here: to move to the side)

der Werkschutz
the security guard

die Werkshalle, -n
the work area

der Werkshof, ⁻e
the factory yard

der Werkzeugmaschinenbau
the factory for the production of machine tools

wirtschaftlich
economical, economically

sich wundern über: Ich wundere mich über die lange Wartezeit.
to be surprised about: I'm surprised about the long waiting time.

das Zelt, -e
the tent

der Zugang, ⁻e: der Zugang zu den Luftwegen (hier: anatomisch)
the entrance, the access: the access to the respiratory tracts (here: anatomically)

die Zunge, -n
the tongue

zurück/fallen (er fällt zurück, ie, a): Die Zunge des Verletzten darf nicht zurückfallen, sonst erstickt er.
to fall back: The injured person's tongue must not fall back, otherwise he will suffocate.

zurück/kehren = zurück/kommen
to return = to come back

die Zusammenarbeit (→ zusammen/arbeiten): die Zusammenarbeit zwischen dem Betriebsrat und der Betriebsleitung
the cooperation: the cooperation between the employees' council and the management

zusammen/kommen (a, o): (= sich versammeln): Heute ist der Betriebsrat zusammengekommen.
to get together (= to gather): The employees' council met today.

zu/schreien D (ie, ie): Er schreit seinem Kollegen zu.
to ye,, to: He yells to his colleague.

zu/stehen D (a, a): Welche Rechte stehen dem Betriebsrat zu?
to be granted: What rights are granted to the council of employees' representatives?

der Zwischenfall, ⁻e
the incident

abenteuerlich: eine abenteuerliche Reise

ab/treiben (ie, ie): Das Boot treibt immer weiter von der Küste ab.

die **Abwechslung, -en:** Wir gehen öfters ins Theater. Wir brauchen diese Abwechslung vom Alltag.

allgemeingültig: eine allgemeingültige Tatsache

an/geben A (er gibt an, a, e): Geben Sie bitte Ihre genaue Position an!

der Angelkutter, —

die **Angst, ⸚e:** Die Kinder haben nachts Angst. Wenn es dunkel wird, bekommen sie es immer mit der Angst zu tun. (= ... werden sie ängstlich.)

Anhalter: Viele junge Leute reisen per Anhalter.

an/knipsen A: Wer hat eben das Licht angeknipst?

an/nehmen A (er nimmt an, a, o): Wir nehmen an, daß ...

der Arbeitsalltag

die Art, -en: ein Boot dieser Art

das **Auge, -n:** Welches Reiseziel haben Sie im Auge?

aus/gehen (i, a): Es ist gut ausgegangen. (= Es ist dabei nichts passiert.)

aus/laufen (er läuft aus, ie, au): Das Schiff ist vor 10 Minuten ausgelaufen.

aus/machen A: Der Kapitän konnte das gesuchte Boot nicht ausmachen.

aus/pumpen A: Dem Patienten wurde der Magen ausgepumpt.

aus/rüsten A: Alle Rettungsboote sind mit einem UKW-Sender ausgerüstet.

ausgebucht sein: Die Hotels sind bereits ausgebucht.

aus/schalten A: Schalten Sie bitte das Licht aus!

außer D: Außer einem Paddel war nichts im Boot.

das Badezeug

in **Bereitschaft** liegen: Die Rettungsboote liegen in Bereitschaft.

besetzt sein: Das Boot war mit drei Personen besetzt.

bestürzt sein: Alle Leute waren über den Unfall bestürzt.

adventurous(ly): an adventurous trip

to **drift off:** The boat drifts farther and farther away from the shore.

the **change:** We go to the theater frequently. We need a change from the everyday routine.

generally valid: a generally valid fact

to **give, to indicate:** Please indicate your exact position.

the fishing cutter

the **fear:** The children are afraid at night. When it becomes dark, they get the jitters. (= ... they become afraid.)

hitchhike: Many young people hitchhike.

to **turn on:** Who just turned on the light?

to **accept, to assume:** We assume that ...

the workday routine

the manner, the kind: a boat of this kind

the **eye:** What destination do you have in mind?

to **go out, to turn out, to end:** it turned out well. (= Nothing terrible happened.)

to **sail:** The ship sailed ten minutes ago.

to **make out:** The captain could not make out the lost boat.

to **pump out:** The patient's stomach was pumped.

to **equip:** All the life boats are equipped with a short-wave radio.

to **be booked fully:** The hotels are already completely booked.

to **turn out:** Please turn out the light!

except for: There was nothing in the boat except for a paddle.

the swim clothes

to **be on stand-by:** The life boats are on stand-by.

to **be occupied:** The boat was occupied by three persons.

to **be aghast:** Everyone was aghast about the accident.

betagt (= alt): eine betagte Dame
betätigen A: Sie können die Ampel betätigen, indem Sie hier auf den Knopf drücken.
bleich: ein bleiches Gesicht
das Boot, -e
breit: Das Boot ist 2,35 Meter breit.
der Bundesdeutsche, -n (umgangssprachlich für:) ein Bürger der Bundesrepublik Deutschland
der Bungalow, -s
der Campingplatz, ⁻e
die Chartermaschine, -n
an/kommen A (a, o): Mir kommt es darauf an, einen ruhigen Urlaubsort zu finden.
das Ding, -er: so ein leichtes Ding wie dieses Boot
der Einsatz: unter Einsatz von Gesundheit und Leben
der **Einsatz**, ⁻e: Der Einsatz des Rettungsboots dauerte zwei Stunden.
die Endstation, -en
entdecken A: Die Kinder wurden von der Polizei in einem kleinen Boot entdeckt.
der **Entschluß**, ⁻(ss)e: Sind Sie schon zu einem Entschluß gekommen?
sich **erholen:** Wie haben Sie sich im Urlaub erholt?
erschöpft sein: Die Leute kamen erschöpft von der Rettungsaktion zurück.
erziehen A (o, o): Ich bin seit meiner Kindheit zur Sparsamkeit erzogen worden.
die Fahrt, in langsamer Fahrt
das Ferienhaus, ⁻er
fiktiv: ein fiktiver Dialog
der Fischkutter, —
flau: mit flauem Magen
frei/schleppen A: Der Kreuzer schleppte das gestrandete Schiff frei.
freiwillig: freiwillige Helfer
fremd: fremde Länder
der Friedhof, ⁻e
frieren (o, o): Wir haben in der Nacht ganz schön gefroren.
der Funkspruch, ⁻e
der Fußgänger, —
die Fußgängerampel, -n
die Geburtswehen (Plural)
die Gegenwart

aged (= old): a lady well advanced in years
to **activate:** You can activate the traffic light by pushing this button here.

pale: a pale face
the boat
wide: The boat is 2.34 meters wide.
the citizen of the Federal Republic of Germany

the bungalow
the camping site
the charter plane
to **matter, to be important:** It is important to me to find a quiet place for my vacation.
the thing, the object: such a light object as this boat
the effort, the risk: at risk of life and health
the **operation:** The operation of the life boat lasted two hours.
the end station, the terminal
to **discover:** The children were discovered by the police in a small boat.
the **decision:** Have you already come to a decision?
to **rest, to relax:** Did you have a restful vacation?
to **be exhausted:** The people returned exhausted from the rescue operation.
to **educate:** I've been taught to be thrifty since my childhood.
the drive, the sail: at slow speed
the vaction house, the summer house
imaginary: an imaginary dialogue
the fishing cutter
weak: with a weak stomach
to **free, to pull afloat, or clear:** The life boat freed the stranded ship.
volunatry: volunteers
foreign: foreign countries
the cemetery
to **be cold, to freeze:** We were really very cold during the night.
the radiogram, the wireless message
the pedestrian
the traffic light
the labor pains
the present

die Geschwindigkeit, -en
der Getriebeschaden, ⸚
gut gehen: Das Geschäft geht gut. (= Das Geschäft floriert.)
Hals über Kopf: Die Leute sind Hals über Kopf abgereist.
die Hauskatze, -n
der Helfer, —
heraus/greifen A (i, i): ein willkürlich herausgegriffener Tag
das Hilfsmittel, —
sich **hinaus/wagen:** Bei diesem Wetter wagt sich niemand aufs Meer hinaus.
hinaus/treiben (ie, ie): Das Boot wurde aufs Meer hinausgetrieben.
Hochbetrieb haben: Im Sommer haben die Reisebüros Hochbetrieb.
in Höhe des Campingplatzes
der Individualist, -en
die Jacht, -en
die Jolle, -n
der Jugendliche, -n
der Kapitän, -e
die Katze, -n
der Katzenjammer: (hier im Doppelsinn:) 1. das Klagen der Katze; 2. die Ernüchterung nach einer durchzechten Nacht (hier: nach einem guten Essen)
keinerlei: Wir haben keinerlei Hilfsmittel.

kentern: Das Boot ist gekentert.
der Knopf, ⸚e (an einer elektrischen Anlage)
Knoten: eine Geschwindigkeit von 10 Knoten; 1 kn = 1 852 m per Stunde
die Küste, -n
die Küstenfunkstelle, -n
das Küstenmotorschiff, -e
die Landseite: von Landseite her
die Länge: eine Länge von 6,92 Meter
lauten: Die Meldung lautet: ...
der **Leichtsinn:** So ein Leichtsinn!

leichtsinnig: leichtsinnige Touristen
sich.**leisten** können A: Wir können uns keine Urlaubsreise leisten.
die Leistung: Die Leistung des Motors liegt bei 45 PS.
manövrierunfähig: ein manövrierunfähiges Schiff

the speed
the size: different sizes
to **go well:** Business is going well. (= Business is flourishing.)
head over heels: The people left in a great hurry.
the house cat
the helper, the assistant
to **choose, to single out:** an arbitrarily chosen day
the resource, the auxiliary means
to **dare to go out:** No one dares to go out to sea in this weather.
to **drift out:** The boat drifted out to sea.
to **be in high season:** In the summer travel agencies have their busy season.
off the camping site
the individualist
the yacht
the dinghy
the youth
the captain
the cat
the hang-over (literally, the cat's wining): (here in a double sense:) 1. the wailing of the cat; 2. the after effects of a night of drinking (here: after a good dinner)
none whatsoever: We have no resources whatsoever.
to **capsize:** The boat capsized.
the button (on a piece of electrical equipment)
knot: a speed of 10 knots; 1 knot = 1 852 meters per hour
the coast, the shore
the coastal radio station
the coastal motorship
the shore: from the shore
the length: a length of 6.92 meters
to **sound, to read:** The message read: ...
the **carelessness, the thoughtlessness:** Such carelessness!
careless(ly): careless tourists
to **be able to afford:** We can't afford to go on vacation.
the performance, the output: The motor has a strength of 45 hp.
incapable of maneuvers: a ship incapable of maneuvers

das Meer, -e

die **Meldung, -en:** Der Kapitän hat von der Küstenfunkstelle eine Meldung erhalten.

der Motorschaden, ⸗

das Motorschiff, -e

munter: eine kleine muntere Katze

naß: unser nasses Badezeug

offen: die offene See

orkanartig: ein orkanartiger Wind

das Paddel, —

die **Pension, -en:** Wir hatten ein Zimmer in einer Pension.

der Pilz, -e: giftige Pilze, eßbare Pilze

planen A: Was haben Sie für Ihren Urlaub geplant?

das Plastikboot, -e

die **Position, -en:** Wie ist die Position des Schiffes?

praktisch unsinkbar: Das Boot ist praktisch unsinkbar.

zur **Rede** stellen A: Der Polizist stellte die Frau zur Rede.

der Reiselustige, -n

auf **Reisen** sein: Dein Vater ist dauernd auf Reisen.

der Reiseveranstalter, —

die Reisezeit

das Reiseziel, -e

retten A: Im vergangenen Jahr sind 166 Personen aus Seenot gerettet worden.

die Rettung, -en

die Rettungschronik, -en

die Rettungsstation, -en

die Rettungsweste, -n

das Rollfeld

sämtlich: Sämtliche Passagiere sind gerettet worden.

schaffnerlos (= ohne Schaffner): eine schaffnerlose Straßenbahn

scheinen (ie, ie): Unser Nachbar scheint auf Reisen zu sein.

die Schiffbrüchige, -n

in **Schlepp** nehmen: Der Fischkutter wurde in Schlepp genommen.

der Schmerz, -en: vor Schmerzen

schwarz/fahren (er fährt schwarz, u, a): Die Kinder sind den ganzen Tag schwarzgefahren.

the sea, the ocean

the **message:** The captain received a message from the coastal radio station.

the engine trouble, the engine failure

the motorship

lively: a small, lively cat

wet: wet swim clothes

open: the open sea

hurricane-like: a hurricane-like wind

the paddle

the **inn:** We had a room in an inn.

the mushroom: poisonous mushrooms, edible mushrooms

to **plan:** What are your vacation plans?

the plastic boat

the **position:** What is the position of the ship?

practically unsinkable: The boat is practically unsinkable.

to **call to account:** The policeman questioned the woman.

the person who likes to travel

to **be on the road:** Your father is always on the road.

the travel agent, the tour organizer

the tourist season

the destination

to **rescue:** Last year 166 persons were rescued from distress at sea.

the rescue

the chronicle of rescue operations

the rescue station

the life jacket

the runway

all, all of them: All of the passengers were rescued.

without a conductor: a streetcar without a conductor

to **appear, to seam:** Our neighbor appears to be on a trip.

the shipwrecked woman

to **tug, to tow:** The fishing cutter was towed.

the pain: in pain

to **ride without a ticket:** The children rode without tickets all day long.

in **Schwierigkeiten** geraten (er gerät, ie, a): Bei dem starken Wind die die Leute in dem Boot in Schwierigkeiten geraten.
to **tun into difficulties:** The people in the boat ran into difficulties due to the strong wind.

der Schwimmer, —
the swimmer

die See: auf See; auf hoher See
the sea, the ocean: at sea; out at sea

die Seefahrt
the nautical mile

der **Seegang:** Heute früh war schwerer Seegang.
the **heavy sea:** There was a heavy sea this morning.

die Seemeile, -n
the nautical mile

in **Seenot** geraten (er gerät, ie, a): Das Motorschiff ist in Seenot geraten.
to **come into distress at sea:** The motorship came into distress at sea.

der Seenotretter, —
the rescuer

der Seenotrettungskreuzer, —
the rescue boat

der **Selbständige**, -n (= jemand der selbständig ist)
the independent person (= someone who is independent)

selbstverständlich
obvious(ly)

in **Sicherheit** bringen A: Die Passagiere sind zuerst in Sicherheit gebracht worden.
to **secure, to bring to safety:** First the passengers were brought to safety.

sichten A: Wir haben auf hoher See einen Fischkutter gesichtet.
to **sight:** We sighted a fishing cutter out at sea.

die Sparsamkeit
the thriftiness

das Sportgeschäft, -e
the sporting goods store

die Sprache, -n: eine andere Sprache sprechen (figurativ: etwas anderes sagen)
the language: to speak another language (figuratively: to say something different)

stationiert sein: Das Rettungsboot ist in Heiligenhafen stationiert.
to **be stationed:** The life boat is stationed in Heiligenhafen.

statistisch
statistical(ly)

stoppen A: Der Polizist stoppte den Verkehr. — Das Schiff stoppte.
to **stop:** The policeman stopped the traffic. — The ship stopped.

stranden: Gestern ist hier ein Motorschiff gestrandet.
to **run aground:** Yesterday a motorship ran aground here.

das Strand-Rettungsboot, -e
the coastal life boat

der Straßenbahnzug, ⁻e
the streetcar

der Streifenwagen, —
the police car

der Sturm, ⁻e
the storm

der Tätigkeitsbericht, -e
the operational report

die Technik
technical science

die Tonne, -n (als Seezeichen im Meer)
the buoy (as a signal at sea)

über: das ganze Jahr über (= während des ganzen Jahres)
over: throughout the whole year (= during the entire year)

über/queren A: Die Frau überquert die Straße.
to **cross:** The woman crosses the street.

überwinden A (a, u): Die Retter mußten viele Gefahren überwinden.
to **overcome:** The rescuers had to overcome many dangers.

UKW-Seefunk = Ultrakurzwelle-Seefunk
short-wave sea transmitter

die Umfrage, -n
the poll

unsinkbar: Das Schiff ist fast unsinkbar.
unsinkable: The ship is almost unsinkable.

unterkühlt sein: Die Leute, die aus dem
to **have a below normal body temperature,**

Wasser gerettet worden sind, waren unterkühlt und mußten ins Krankenhaus gebracht werden.

unternehmen A (er unternimmt, a, o): Der Kapitän hat heute schon zwei Rettungsaktionen unternommen.

unterschätzen A: Die Touristen unterschätzen die Gefahr auf See.

unvorsichtig: ein unvorsichtiger Schwimmer

der Urlauber, —

verfrachten A: Die Leute wurden alle auf Lastkraftwagen verfrachtet.

zur **Verfügung** stehen D: Hier stehen zwei Rettungsboote zur Verfügung.

die Vergangenheit

sich **vergiften**: Hat sich die Katze vergiftet?

verkehrsbehindernd: ein verkehrsbehinderndes Verhalten

sich **verkriechen** (o, o): Die Katze hat sich unter das Bett verkrochen.

vermißt: Ein Kind ist als vermißt gemeldet worden.

die Vermutung, -en (vermuten A)

verspüren A: Er verspürte einen Schmerz im Magen.

sich **wälzen**: Das Tier wälzte sich vor Schmerzen am Boden.

werfen A (er wirft, a, o): Die Katze hat fünf Junge geworfen.

willkürlich

der Wind, -e

wortlos: Er verließ wortlos das Zimmer.

der Zebrastreifen, -n (bei einem Fußgängerübergang)

sich **zeigen**: Ob wir Glück haben, wird sich bald zeigen.

der Zeitbezug, ̈-e: ohne Zeitbezug

die Zeitdauer

der Zeitpunkt

ziemlich: Nach der Rettungsaktion waren alle ziemlich erschöpft.

die Zukunft

die Zwischenzeit: in der Zwischenzeit

to be undercooled: The people who were rescued from the water were undercooled and had to be brought to the hospital.

to **attempt, to undertake:** Today the captain has already undertaken two rescue operations.

to **underestimate:** The tourists underestimate the danger at sea.

careless, negligent: an imprudent swimmer

the vacationer

to **load, to put on:** The people were all loaded onto trucks.

to **be at s. o.'s disposal:** Two lifeboats are available.

the past

to **poison o. s.:** Was the cat poisoned?

traffic-impeding: traffic-impeding behavior

to **hide, to crawl away:** The cat hid under the bed.

missing: A child has been reported missing.

the presumption

to **feel, to notice:** He felt a pain in the stomach.

to **roll:** The animal rolled on the floor in pain.

to **throw:** The cat gave birth to five kittens.

arbitrary, arbitrarily

the wind

without a word: He left the room without a word.

the pedestrian crossing (at a crosswalk)

to **show itself:** We'll soon find out whether we're in luck.

the time reference: without time reference

the time period

the moment

quite, rather: Everyone was quite exhausted after the rescue operation.

the future

the meantime: in the meantime

ab und zu: Wir gehen ab und zu ins Theater.

ab/bauen A: Im Sport kann man seine Aggressionen abbauen.

abstiegsbedroht: eine abstiegsbedrohte Fußballmannschaft (= eine Fußballmannschaft, die aufgrund schlechter Ergebnisse davon bedroht ist, aus der Bundesliga in die Regionalliga absteigen zu müssen)

die Aggression, -en

sich **aktiv** betätigen: Wir betätigen uns aktiv im Sport.

die Alltagssorgen (Plural)

der Alltagsstreß

anderthalb Stunden = eineinhalb Stunden

an/fangen: Er weiß nichts mit seiner Zeit anzufangen.

angeschlossen (→ anschließen): Unser Verein ist dem Sportclub angeschlossen.

angestaut (→ an/stauen): angestaute Aggressionen

an/halten (er hält an, ie, a): Unser Erfolg hält auch bei den nächsten Spielen an.

sich **anpassen:** Sie müssen sich der Situation anpassen.

an/regen: Schwimmen ist ein Sport, der den Blutkreislauf anregt.

die Anregung, -en

anthropologisch

die Après-Ski-Bekanntschaft, -en: eine Bekanntschaft, die man wörtlich: nach dem Skifahren gemacht hat

argumentieren

die Art: Möglichkeiten aller Art

auf/spielen: Bei den Meisterschaftsspielen spielte der Verein gut auf. (aufspielen hier: gleichbedeutend mit spielen)

der Aufwärtstrend: einen Aufwärtstrend nehmen (= erfolgreicher werden)

das Auge, -n: vor unseren Augen

aus/brechen (er bricht aus, a, o): Viele Menschen versuchen aus ihrer Situation auszubrechen.

der Ausflug, ⁀e: (hier: der Spazierflug = ein Flug ohne ein bestimmtes Ziel)

once in a while: We go to the theater once in a while.

to **discharge:** Aggressions can be discharged in sports.

threatened with decline: a soccer team threatened with reduction of its status (= a soccer team which is threatened with a reduction of its status from the National League to the Regional League because of bad scores)

the aggression

to **be active:** We participate actively in sports.

the worries of everyday life

the stress of everyday life

one and a half hours

to **begin:** He doesn't know what to do with his time.

affiliated: Our association is affiliated with the sports club.

pent-up: pent-up aggressions

to **continue:** Our success will continue in the coming games.

to **adjust to:** You have to adjust to the situation.

to **stimulate:** Swimming is a sport which stimulates the circulation.

the stimulation, the suggestion

anthropological(ly)

the after-skiing-acquaintance: an acquaintance made literally after a day of skiing

to argue

the manner, the kind: possibilities of all kinds

to **perform:** The club performed well in the National League Tournament. (to perform here: equivalent in meaning with to play)

the trend upwards: to be on the way up (= to become more successful)

the eye: in front of our eyes

to **escape, to break out:** Many people try to break out of their situations.

the escursion: (here: the excursion flight = a flight without a fixed destination)

die Ausflugschneise, -n (Gegensatz: die Anflugschneise) = der Teil des Luftraums über einem Flugplatz, der einem Flugzeug zum Abflug zugewiesen wird

the exit corridor (opposite: the entrance corridor) = the part of the air space above an airport which is assigned to an airplane for departure

aus/lassen A (er läßt aus, ie, a): Wir lassen keine Gelegenheit aus, auf den Sportplatz zu gehen.

to **leave out, to miss:** We don't miss a single opportunity to go to the sports field.

die **Aussicht:** Unser Verein hat die besten Aussichten, das Spiel zu gewinnen.

the **prospect:** Our club has the best prospects for winning the game.

die Auswirkung, -en
the effect

die Autobahn, -en
the highway

der Bahnsteig, -e
the platform at the railroad station

das Basteln (→ basteln = in der Freizeit kleinere handwerkliche Arbeiten tun)
to do crafts as a hobby (= to do small craft projects in spare time)

beanspruchen A: Wir beanspruchen unser volles Recht.
to **demand:** We demand all of our rights.

beliebt: ein beliebtes Ferienziel
popular: a popular vacation destination

der Berg, -e
the mountain

der Berufsärger (= der Ärger, den man im Beruf hat)
the troubles on the job (= the troubles which one has in professional life)

die Beständigkeit
the continuance, the perseverence

bestehen: Bestehen noch Aussichten, daß wir das Spiel gewinnen?
to **exist, to be:** Do we still have a chance to win the game?

betrachten: Ihr könnt euch schon als Sieger betrachten.
to **consider:** You can already consider yourselves winners.

beweisen: Sie müssen mir das erst beweisen, sonst glaube ich das nicht.
to **prove:** You have to prove that to me first, otherwise I won't believe it.

die Bildungsmöglichkeit, -en
the possibility of, or for, education

der Blutkreislauf
the circulation

brauchen: Heute brauchen wir nicht zu arbeiten.
to **need:** We don't have to work today.

das Briefmarkensammeln → Briefmarken sammeln
stamp collecting

die Bundesliga, -ligen
the National League

die **Chance:** Wir hatten keine Chance, das Spiel zu gewinnen.
the **chance:** We didn't have a chance to win the game.

der Charakter, die Charaktere
the character

dabei: Ihr wollt nicht spazieren gehen. Und dabei ist das Wetter heute so schön.
just: You don't want to take a walk. And just today the weather is so lovely.

der Derby-Sieg, -e
the derby victory

die Disziplin, -en (im Sport)
specific kind (of sport)

Do-it-yourself = Heimwerkern (als Laie im Hause handwerkliche Arbeiten ausführen)
do-it-yourself = being a handy-man (to do repairs and building around the house as an amateur craftsman)

drin: Bei unserem kommenden Spiel ist durchaus noch ein Sieg drin. (= Wir haben bei dem kommenden Spiel durchaus noch die Chance zu gewinnen.)
within it, possible: A victory is still possible in our upcoming game. (= We still have a very good chance to win the upcoming game.)

durch/machen A: Unser Verein hat eine schwere Zeit durchgemacht.

sich **durch/setzen**: Auf die Dauer wird sich unser Sportverein durchsetzen.

die **Durststrecke**: In der letzten Spielsaison hat unser Verein eine Durststrecke durchgemacht. (= figurativ: ... hat unser Verein keine Erfolge gehabt.)

eben: Das Fußballspielen macht uns eben Spaß.

echt (salopp für: wirklich)

ein/holen A: Wir haben mit unserem letzten Sieg euren Verein eingeholt.

sich **ein/stellen** auf A: Wir müssen uns jetzt auf eine Niederlage einstellen.

entbehrungsreich: ein entbehrungsreiches Leben

enorm

entgegen/sehen (er sieht entgegen, a, e): Wir sehen jetzt einem entscheidenden Spiel entgegen. (= Wir erwarten jetzt ein entscheidendes Spiel.)

entnehmen aus (er entnimmt, a, o) = erkennen an

sich **entspannen**: Entspannen Sie sich vor dem Spiel.

die Erfahrung, -en

der Erfolg, -e

erheben (o, o): Er hat den Zeigefinger erhoben. (= Er hat gewarnt.)

der Europacup

das Exclusivrecht, -e

das Ferienhaus, -̈er

die **Ferse, -n**: Euer Verein ist uns hart auf den Fersen. (= Euer Verein folgt uns unmittelbar.)

die Fieberkurve, -n

fit sein (im Sport)

die Fliegerei

die Form: in guter Form (sportlich)

der Formel-I-Wagen, —

der Fortschritt, -e

sich frei bewegen

die Freizeit

fremd: ein fremder Mann

das Freundschaftsspiel (beim Fußball)

frisch sein (körperlich)

früher

die Gegebenheit, -en (= die Situation, -en)

to **go through**: Our club has been through a hard time.

to **succeed**: In the long run our sports club will succeed.

the **slump**: Our club went through a slump during the last season. (figuratively: ... our club had no victories.)

just, plain: Playing soccer is plain fun for us.

genuine: (everyday language for: really)

to **catch up**: We caught up with your club by our last victory.

to **prepare o.s. for, to get ready for**: Now we have to prepare ourselves for a defeat.

deprived: an ascetic life

enormous(ly)

to **look forward to, to anticipate**: Now we're anticipating a decisive game. (= Now we're expecting a decisive game.)

to realize from = to recognize by

to **relax**: Relax before the game.

the experience

the success

to **raise, to lift**: He raised his forefinger in warning. (= He warned.)

The European Cup

the exclusive right

the vacation house, the summer house

the **heel**: Your club is hard on our heels. (= Your club is directly behind us.)

the temperature chart

to be fit (in sports)

the aviation

the shape: in good shape (athletic)

the Type-I racing car

the progress

to move freely

the leisure time

strange, unknown: a stranger

the exhibition game (in soccer)

to be vigorous (physiologically)

earlier, before, in earlier times

the circumstance (= the situation)

der Geist: sportlicher Geist — the spirit: athletic spirit
gelingen (a, u): Es ist gelungen, ... — to **succeed**: We succeeded ...
gemessen an D = Im Vergleich mit — compared with = in comparison with
das Geschlecht, -er: das schwache Geschlecht (= die Frauen) — the sex: the fair sex (= women)
die Gesellschaft: die moderne Gesellschaft — the society: the modern society
gesund — healthy
gewandelt: die gewandelte Rolle = die veränderte Rolle — changed: the changed role = the transformed role
der Gleichgesinnte, -n (einer, der die gleiche Gesinnung/Ansicht hat) — the like-minded person (a person who has the same convictions and views)
der Glückwunsch, -̈e — the congratulations
der Gott, -̈er: Grüß Gott! — the Lord: Greetings!
halt = eben — after all
hart: ein harter Sport — tough: a tough sport
sich wie zu **Hause** fühlen: Wir fühlen uns hier wie zu Hause. — to feel at **home**: We feel at home here.
heikel: eine heikle Aufgabe — delicate, difficult: a delicate task
die Heimat — the homeland
der Herr der Schöfung (figurativ für: die Männer) — the lord of creation (figuratively for: the men)
der Himmel — the sky
hinaus/schauen: Die Leute schauen aus dem Fenster hinaus. — to **look out:** The people look out of the window.
hintereinander (= einer nach dem anderen) — after one another (= one after the other)
das Hobby, die Hobbies — the hobby
holen: den Europacup holen = gewinnen — to fetch, to get: to receive the European Cup = to win

die Insel, -n — the island
international — international(ly)
das Interview, -s — the interview
das Jahr, -e: von Jahr zu Jahr — the year: from year to year
die Judomatte, -en — the judo mat
der Kaffeeflug, -̈e: hier: ein Spazierflug, um am Zielort Kaffee zu trinken — the coffee flight: here: an excursion flight for the purpose of drinking coffee at the destination
kämpfen (im Sport) — to fight (in sports)
die Kontrollzone, -n: die Zone, die vom Tower aus kontrolliert wird — the control zone: the zone which is controlled from the tower
sich **konzentrieren** auf A: Ich muß mich auf meine Arbeit konzentrieren. — to **concentrate on:** I have to concentrate on my job.
der Kopilot, -en — the copilot
die Kraft, -̈e — the strength
der Kreis: im Kreise der Familie = in der Familie — the circle: with the family = in the family
künftig: ein künftiger Sportflieger — future: a future sports aviator
laufen (er läuft, ie, au): Es läuft alles nach Wunsch. — to **run:** Everything is going according to plan.
die Leichtathletik — the track and field sports
die Leistungsdifferenz, -en — the difference in performance (achievement)

die Leistungskurve (im Sport)	the performance record
liegen: Die Zahl der Mitglieder liegt bei rund 18 000 Personen.	to **lie:** The membership is around 18,000 persons.
das Linienflugzeug, -e	the commercial airplane
mahnen: der mahnende Zeigefinger	to remind, to warn: the forefinger raised in warning
die **Männersache:** Viele betrachten den Fußballsport als reine Männersache.	**something only for men:** Many regard the game of soccer as strictly men's business.
die Mannschaft, -en	the team
die Marathonstrecke, -n	the marathon stretch
messen (er mißt, a, e): Die Mädchen messen mit den Jungen ihre Kräfte.	to **measure, to match:** The girls measure their strength with that of the boys.
mit/mischen (umgangssprachlich für: beteiligt sein an A)	to get in: everyday language for: to participate in
der Moment, -e	the moment
momentan	at the moment
der Motorflugverein, -e	the motor aviation club
die Muskulatur	the muscular system
nach der Theorie	according to theory
nach/eifern D: Die Mädchen eifern den Jungen nach.	to **emulate:** The girls emulate the boys.
die **Nachfrage:** Danke der Nachfrage!	the **inquiry:** Thanks for asking!
die Naturverbundenheit	the love of nature
neulich	the other day
die Neuorientierung	the reorientation
die Niederlage, -n (im Sport)	the defeat (in sports)
notieren A = registrieren A	to note = to register
nutzen A: seine Zeit nutzen	to use: to make use of his time
sich organisieren (in einem Verein)	to get organized (in a club)
der Personalchef, -s	the director of personnel
der Platz, "-e: den Platz halten (im Sport)	the place: to keep one's rank (in sports)
der Privatpilot, -en	the pilot of a private plane
der Prozeß, -(ss)e (= die Entwicklung, -en)	the process (= the development)
registrieren A	to register
die **Reiselust:** Im Sommer herrscht große Reiselust unter den Menschen.	the **desire to travel:** People have a great desire to travel in the summertime.
der **Reiz, -e:** Der Wintersport hat auch seine Reize.	the **charm, the attraction:** Winter sports are also attractive.
revidieren A = korrigieren A	to revise = to correct
die Romantik	the romanticism
die Rückkehr (→ zurück/kehren)	the return
das Segelboot, -e	the sailing boat
selbst = sogar	even
die Serie, -n: die Erfolgsserie	the series: the series of victories
schauen: Er schaut aus dem Fenster.	to **look:** He looks out of the window.
beim **Schopf** packen A: Wir müssen die Gelegenheit beim Schopf packen.	to **seize:** We have to seize the opportunity.
schwach	weak(ly)
die Sicht: klare Sicht	the visibility: good visibility

der Sieger, —	the winner
sinnvoll	sensible, sensibly
sogenannt	so-called
die Sonn- und Feiertage (Plural): an Sonn- und Feiertagen	the Sundays and holidays: on Sundays and holidays
der **Spaß:** Die Fliegerei macht Spaß.	the **fun:** Flying is fun.
der Spazierflug, ̈-e (= ein Flug ohne ein bestimmtes Ziel)	the excursion flight (= a flight without a fixed destination)
der Spitzensport	the championship sports
der **Sport:** Treiben Sie Sport?	**sports:** Do you go in for sports?
der Sportbegeisterte, -n (= einer, der sich für Sport begeistern kann)	the sports enthusiast (= a person who can be enthusiastic about sports)
die Sportdisziplin, -en (= die Sportarten)	the kind of sport
die Sportfliegerei	the sports aviation
der Sprung: auf dem Sprung sein = dabei sein, etwas zu tun (Wir sind gerade auf dem Sprung, ins Theater zu gehen.)	the jump: to be at the point of = to be just about to do something (We're just about to go to the theater.)
das Stadion, die Stadien	the stadium
stark sein (hier: fit sein)	to be strong (here: to be fit)
das **Steckenpferd, -e:** Er hat die Fliegerei als Steckenpferd.	the **hobby:** Aviation is his hobby.
stehen: stehender Verkehr	to stand: traffic at a standstill
steigen (ie, ie): Die Zahl unserer Mitglieder ist gestiegen.	to **climb, to increase:** Our membership has increased.
das **Steuer, —:** Wer sitzt dort am Steuer?	the **steering wheel:** Who's at the wheel there?
das Symptom, -e	the symptom
die Theorie, -n	the theory
der Titel, —	the title
der Tower, —	the tower
traditionell	traditional(ly)
der Trainer, —	the trainer
die Treibstoffmenge, -n	the quantity of gasoline
tun: Gestern hatte ich den ganzen Tag nichts zu tun.	to **do:** Yesterday I had nothing to do all day long.
überzeugt sein von: Wir sind nicht von deinen Leistungen überzeugt.	to **be convinced of,** or **by:** We're not convinced by your achievements.
unhaltbar: eine unhaltbare Theorie	untenable: an untenable theory
der Verein, -e	the club, the association
verdienen A: Ich weiß nicht, ob das Autofahren das Wort „Sport" verdient.	to **merit:** I don't know whether car driving merits the term "sport".
verlaufen (er verläuft, ie, au): Das Spiel verlief gut.	to **take its course:** The game turned out well.
vermessen sein: Er war so vermessen zu behaupten, daß ...	to **be audacious:** He was audacious enough to maintain that ...
verstopft: verstopfte Straßen	congested: congested streets
der Vogel, ̈-	the bird
die Vogelperspektive	the bird's-eye view
sich **vollziehen** (o, o): Es vollzieht sich ein Prozeß der Emanzipation.	to **take place:** An emancipation process is taking place.

von ... an: von nun an
vorn: Unser Verein ist ganz vorn. (= Unser Verein gehört zu den Besten.)
vor/schreiben (ie, ie) der vorgeschriebene Weg
weitaus: Schwimmen ist weitaus gesünder als Autofahren.
der Wille
der Winter, –
die Wintertemperatur, -en
wohlauf sein: Wir sind alle wohlauf.
die Zeit: zur Zeit; wir finden keine Zeit für ein Hobby
der Zeigefinger, –
das Zeug: Du hast das Zeug für einen guten Sportler.
der Zuschauer, –
zweitrangig: ein zweitrangiger Verein

from ... on: from now on
in front: Our club is way out front. (= Our club is one of the best.)
to prescribe: the prescribed path
far more: Swimming ist far more healthy than car driving.
the will, the determination
the winter
the winter temperature
to be well: We are all well.
the time: at this time; we have no time for a hobby
the forefinger
the stuff: You have the makings of a good athlete.
the spectator
second-class: a second-class club

Abschnitt 9

der Abendbummel: Wollen wir jetzt noch einen kleinen Abendbummel machen?
ab/schätzen A: Kannst du abschätzen, wieviel alle Sachen zusammen kosten?
das Altertum
sich ändern: In den letzten Jahren hat sich hier in der Stadt vieles geändert.
angemessen: ein angemessenes Trinkgeld
angrenzend: angrenzende Orte
an/raunzen A: Der Mann hat mich angeraunzt. (= Der Mann hat mich unfreundlich angesprochen.)
an/schaffen A: Habt ihr ein neues Fernsehgerät angeschafft?
anscheinend: Die Kinovorstellung ist anscheinend schon zu Ende.
an/sprechen A (er spricht an, a, o): Auf der Straße hat mich jemand angesprochen.
die Anzahlung, -en (→ an/zahlen A): Die Anzahlung für den Wagen habe ich heute auf Ihr Konto überwiesen.
auf/klären A: Darf ich das Mißverständnis aufklären?
auf/nehmen A (er nimmt auf, a, o): Nehmen Sie mit der Firma Kontakt auf!

the evening stroll: Shall we take a little evening stroll now?
to estimate: Can you estimate how much everything costs?
antiquity
to change: Many things have changed in the city in recent years.
appropriate: an appropriate tip
adjoining: adjoining towns
to grumble: The man grumbled at me. (= The man spoke to me in an unfriendly manner.)
to buy, to purchase: Have you bought a new television set?
apparent(ly): Apparently the movie is over.
to speak to, to address: Someone spoke to me on the street.
the downpayment: Today I transferred the downpayment for the car to your account.
to clear up, to explain: May I clear up this misunderstanding?
to take up: Make contact with the company!

auf/passen: Passen Sie auf, ob die Rechnung stimmt!

auf/weisen A (ie, ie): Kaum eine Stadt weist eine so belebte Straße auf wie den Kurfürstendamm in Berlin.

aus/geben A (er gibt aus, a, e): Wieviel Geld hast du für die Reise ausgegeben?

sich **aus/kennen:** Kennen Sie sich hier in der Stadt aus?

aus/lösen A: Der laute Straßenverkehr löst bei den Leuten den Wunsch aus, außerhalb der Stadt zu wohnen.

aus/machen A: Es macht einen Unterschied von nur einer Ziffer aus, ob ...

die Ausnahme, -n: die Ausnahme von der Regel

barsch: mit barscher Stimme

begegnen: Ich bin niemandem auf der Straße begegnet.

beklemmend: eine beklemmende Stille

belebt: eine belebte Straße

belehren: Er belehrte mich, daß ... (= Er erklärte mir, daß ...)

die Bewegung, -en

brieflich: eine briefliche Nachricht

britisch

das Bundesgebiet = das Gebiet der Bundesrepublik Deutschland

die Bürozeit, -en

die City = die Innenstadt

der Doppeltriller (als Telefonzeichen)

durch/führen A: einen Test durchführen

die Eigentumswohnung, -en

einst = früher

die Einwohnerschaft

der Entschuldigungsbrief, -e

die Entwicklung, -en

die Erbschaft, -en

der Erball (= der Globus)

erfordern A: Es gibt Sportarten, die sehr viel Mut erfordern.

sich **ergeben:** Was hat sich aus der Umfrage ergeben?

erheblich = bedeutend

sich **erkundigen** nach: Ich wollte mich nach Ihren Wünschen erkundigen.

ernst nehmen A: Ich nehme die Sache sehr ernst.

erreichbar sein: Ich bin jederzeit telefonisch erreichbar.

to **pay attention, to watch out:** Check and see if the bill is correct!

to **show:** Hardly any city boasts such a lively street as the Kurfürstendamm in Berlin.

to **spend:** How much money did you spend for the trip?

to **know the way around:** Do you know your way around the city?

to **trigger, to release:** The noisy street traffic makes the people want to live outside the city.

to **matter:** There is a difference of only one number, whether ...

the exception: the exception from the rule

unfriendly: with an unfriendly voice

to **encounter, to meet:** I didn't meet anybody on the street.

oppressive: an oppressive silence

lively: a lively street

to **enlighten, to teach:** He showed me that ... (= He explained to me that ...)

the movement

written: a written message

British

the Federal area = the area of the Federal Republic of Germany

the office hours

the city = the inner city

the double trill (as a telephone signal)

to carry out: to carry out a test

the condominium

once = some time ago

the inhabitants, the population

the letter of apology

the development

the inheritance

the earth (= the globe)

to **demand:** There are types of sports which demand a lot of courage.

to **result:** What were the results of the poll?

considerable, considerably = significant(ly)

to **inquire about:** I wanted to inquire about your wishes.

to **take seriously:** I take this matter very seriously.

to **be within reach:** You can reach me on the phone at any time.

fehlen D: Mir fehlt die Zeit, mich mit einem Hobby zu beschäftigen.

flott: ein flotter Wagen
flüchtig: Ich kenne Herrn Müller nur flüchtig.
die Form, -en
fortschreitend: die fortschreitende Entwicklung
der Fortschritt, -e
Fragen stellen D: Du stellst mir wirklich neugierige Fragen.
fremd: Ich bin hier fremd.
sich **Gedanken** machen über A: Machen Sie sich keine Gedanken über Ihre Zukunft!
das Gefühl, -e
das Gespräch, -e
der Gesprächspartner, —
gewinnen A (a, o): Ich habe in der Lotterie gewonnen.
her/bekommen A (a, o): Wie haben Sie Ihre schweren Koffer vom Bahnhof herbekommen?
immerhin: Gehen wir jetzt zum Essen, oder nicht? Es ist immerhin Mittag.
intelligent: ein intelligenter Mensch
die Innenstadt, ⁀e
irgendwo: Ich habe meinen Paß irgendwo liegengelassen.
Jahr: Jahr für Jahr = jedes Jahr
der Kanadier, —
keinesfalls = auf keinen Fall
die Kellnerin, -nen
klick (ein Geräuschwort)
klingen (a, u): Seine Stimme klang sehr freundlich.
der **Kontakt, -e:** Ich suche Kontakte mit einigen deutschen Firmen.
die Konsequenz, -en
der Landkreis, -e
der Lebensrhythmus
die Lotterie, -n
das Lotto
die Männerstimme, -n
die Marktforschung, -en
meinetwegen (hier: zum Beispiel)
die Meinung, -en
sich **melden:** Wer hat sich am Telefon gemeldet?

to **be missing, to be lacking:** I don't have any time to occupy myself with a hobby.
snappy: a snappy car
fleeting(ly): I only know Mr. Müller superficially.
the form
continuing: the continuing development
the progress
to **ask questions:** You're really asking me curious questions.
strange: I'm new here.
to **worry:** Don't worry about your future!

the feeling
the conversation
the conversation partner
to **win:** I won the lottery.

to **get here:** How did you get your heavy suitcase here from the station?

after all: Are we going to lunch now or not? After all, it's noon.
intelligent: an intelligent person
the city
somewhere: I left my passport somewhere.

the year: year after year = every year
the Canadian
in no case
the waitress
click (an onomatopoetic word)
to **sound:** His voice sounded very friendly.

the **contact:** I'm looking for contacts with some German companies.
the consequence
the rural district
the rhythm of life
the lottery
the lottery
the male voice
the market research
if you will (here: for example)
the opinion
to **answer:** Who answered the telephone?

menschlich	human(ly)
die **Miene** verziehen (o, o): Er verzog keine Miene, als ich ihn grüßte.	to **show expression:** He didn't show any expression when I greeted him.
das Ministerium, die Ministerien	the ministry, the government department
die Mischung, -en	the mixture
das Mißverständnis, -se	the misunderstanding
die **Morgenstunde**, -n: In den Morgenstunden ist es schon ziemlich kühl.	the **morning hour:** It's already rather cool in the morning hours.
die Nähe: menschliche Nähe	the proximity: human proximity
natürlich	natural(ly)
nervös	nervous(ly)
der Notizblock, ⸚e	the note pad
die Null, -en	the zero
das Oboenvibrato	the vibrato of the oboe
der Passant, -en	the passer-by
peinlich: eine peinliche Situation	embarrassing: an embarrassing situation
persönlich: Ich kenne ihn nicht persönlich.	**personal(ly):** I don't know him personally.
die **Pforte**, -n: Das Theater hat jetzt seine Pforten für immer geschlossen.	the **gate:** The theater has now closed its gates forever.
der Postweg, -e (= der Weg, den eine Postsendung geht)	the postal route (= the route which a mailing takes)
pulsieren: das pulsierende Leben einer Großstadt	to pulsate: the pulsating life of a large city
rein: ein reines Verkaufszentrum	pure(ly): a district only for shopping
der Rentner, —	the retired person
der **Rubel:** Der Rubel rollt. = Es werden Geschäfte gemacht.	the **ruble:** The ruble rolls. = Business is good.
der Rufton (im Telefon)	the signal (on the telephone)
in **Ruhe** lassen A: Lassen Sie mich jetzt in Ruhe!	to **leave in peace:** Leave me alone now!
sagen: Sagen wir mal ... = Nehmen wir einmal an, ...	to **say:** Let's say ... = Let's assume ...
der Schaufensterbummel	the window-shopping
sehen: Ich sehe die Sache etwas anders als Sie. = Ich beurteile die Sache etwas anders als Sie.	to **see:** I look at the matter somewhat different than you. = I judge the matter somehow differently than you.
sein: Es könnte ja sein. = Es wäre ja möglich.	to **be:** It could well be. = It would be possible.
simpel = einfach	simple
die Sorgen (Plural)	the worries
spaßig: eine spaßige Situation	funny: a funny situation
spielen: Spielen Sie in der Lotterie?	to **play:** Do you play the lottery?
der Stadtbewohner, —	the inhabitant of a city
der Stadtkreis, -e	the city district
die Stadtmitte	the center of town
die Stille: beklemmende Stille	the silence: oppressive silence
die Stimmung, -en	the mood
der Straßenzug, ⸚e	the street
der/das Toto	the toto (lottery for soccer games)
das Trinkgeld, -er	the tip

übrig/bleiben D (er bleibt übrig, ie, ie): Wieviel Geld ist uns nach dem Einkauf noch übriggeblieben?

to remain, to be left over: How much money did we have left over after shopping?

die **Umfrage, -n:** Ein Marktforschungsinstitut will eine Umfrage über Verbraucherwünsche veranstalten (= machen).

the **poll:** An institute for market research wants to conduct a poll about consumer wishes.

das Umland (= das Gebiet um einen bestimmten Ort)

the surrounding area (= the area around a certain town)

unfreiwillig

involuntary, involuntarily

unmittelbar

immediate(ly), direct(ly)

der Unterschied, -e

the difference

die Ursache, -n

the cause

der Verbraucherwunsch, ¨e

the consumer wish

die Verbundenheit

the bond, the tie, the relationship

die Vergnügungsstätte, -n

the places of entertainment

verjubeln A: Er verjubelt sein ganzes Geld.

to **squander:** He blows all his money.

verlegen: eine verlegene Frage

embarrassed: an embarrassed question

verleiten A zu: Die Reklame will die Leute zum Kauf verleiten.

to **induce:** The advertisement is supposed to induce the people to buy.

die Verödung: die Verödung der Städte

the desolation: the desolation of the cities

versehentlich = durch ein Versehen

inadvertent(ly) = by mistake

die Verspätung, -en: mit Verspätung

the delay: with delay

das Verwaltungszentrum, die Verwaltungszentren

the administrative center

vor/kommen D (a, o): Diese Sache kommt mir komisch vor.

to **seem, to appear:** This matter seems strange to me.

die Vorwahl (= die Vorwahlnummer beim Telefon)

the area code (= the area code for telephoning)

wachsen (er wächst, u, a): Die Bevölkerung dieser Stadt ist in den letzten Jahren gewachsen.

to **grow, to increase:** The population of this city has increased in recent years.

die Wählscheibe, -n (am Telefon)

the dial (on the telephone)

der Weg, -e: auf diesem Wege (= auf diese Weise)

the way: in this way (= in this manner)

weiter/gehen (i, a): Die Verödung der Städte geht weiter.

to **continue:** The desolation of the cities continues.

weitreichend: weitreichende Konsequenzen

far-reaching: far-reaching consequences

wesentlich = bedeutend

substantial(ly) = significant(ly)

wieso? = warum?

how? = why?

der Wohnort, -e

the home, the place of residence

der Wunsch, ¨e

the wish, the desire, the demand

wunschlos glücklich (= ohne Wünsche)

entirely satisfied (= without wishes)

die Zeche, -n (= die Geldsumme, die man in einem Restaurant für Essen und Trinken zahlen muß)

the bill (= the sum of money which has to be paid in a restaurant for eating and drinking)

zentrifugal: eine zentrifugale Bewegung

centrifugal(ly): a centrifugal movement

zerknüllen A: Wer hat die neueste Zeitung zerknüllt?

to **crumple:** Who crumpled up the latest newspaper?

zusammen/rechnen A: Rechne mal zusammen, was wir gegessen haben!

to **add up:** Add up what we ate!

Abschnitt 10

ab: ab dem 18. Lebensjahr
ab/bauen A: Es ist schwer, bestehende Vorurteile abzubauen.
sich **ab/finden** mit (a, u): Mit den Schwierigkeiten im Leben muß man sich abfinden.
ab/geben A (er gibt ab, a, e): Hast du (bei der heutigen Wahl) schon deine Stimme abgegeben?
der Abgeordnete, -n
der Abgeordnetensitz, -e (im Parlament)
ab/laufen (er läuft ab, ie, au): Die Legislaturperiode des jetzigen Bundestags läuft im Herbst ab.
ab/lenken A: Laßt euch nicht von der Arbeit ablenken.
ab/nehmen D + A (er nimmt ab, a, o): Der Pfarrer nimmt die Beichte ab.
der Aktenstoß, ⁻e
die Alibifunktion
allgemein: eine allgemeine Wahl
der Alltag
die Amtshandlung, -en
anfangs = am Anfang
sich **an/gewöhnen** A: Gewöhne dir nicht das Rauchen an!
an/kreuzen A: Die Partei, die Sie wählen wollen, müssen Sie auf dem Stimmzettel ankreuzen.
die Ansicht, -en: Ich bin der Ansicht, daß ...
der Applaus: donnernder Applaus
die Arbeitsleistung
das Arbeitsprogramm, -e
arbeitsreich: ein arbeitsreiches Leben
ahnen A: Ich habe geahnt, daß ...
das **Aufarbeiten** → auf/arbeiten: Ich muß nach dem Urlaub die liegengebliebenen Akten aufarbeiten.
auf/erlegen D + A: Der Pfarrer hat der Frau eine Buße auferlegt.
die **Aufgabe** → auf/geben (er gibt auf, a, e): Meine Frau hat ihren Beruf aufgegeben.

from: from the age of 18 on
to **reduce, to eliminate:** It's difficult to eliminate existing prejudices.
to **reconcile o. s. with:** One must reconcile oneself to the difficulties of life.

to **hand in:** Have you already voted (in today's election)?

the parliamentary representative
the seat (in parliament)
to **come to an end:** The legislative term of the present parliament comes to an end in the fall.
to **divert:** Don't let yourselves be diverted from the job.
to **take off:** The priest hears the confession.

the pile of documents
the role of an alibi, the alibi function
general(ly): a general election
the everyday routine
the official function
at (in) the beginning
to **become accustomed to:** Don't get into the habit of smoking!
to **check, to cross:** You have to make a check on the ballot next to the party you want to vote for.
the viewpoint, the opinion: It's my opinion that ...
the applause: thundering applause
the achievement, the performance
the work program
laborious: a laborious life
to **suspect:** I suspected that ...
to **clear up:** After vacation I have to clear up the remaining files.

to **impose:** The priest imposed a penance on the woman.
the **relinquishment:** My wife gave up her job.

auf/räumen A: Heute muß ich die Wohnung aufräumen.

to tidy up: Today I have to tidy up the apartment.

aus/sehen (er sieht aus, a, e): Wie sieht Ihr Reformplan aus?

to appear: What is your plan for reform?

bedenken A: Wenn man bedenkt, daß ...

to consider: If one considers that ...

die Beichte, -n

the confession

beichten: Der Junge geht heute beichten.

to confess: The boy is going to confession today.

der Beichtstuhl, ¨e

the confessional

bekleiden A: Der Minister bekleidete das Amt schon seit zehn Jahren.

to occupy, to hold: The minister has already held the office for ten years.

benommen: benommen vor Freude

confused, benumbed: stupified with joy

bereit/stehen (a, a): Der Kaffee steht schon bereit.

to be ready: The coffee is ready.

besetzt sein: Ist dieser Stuhl besetzt?

to be occupied: Is this seat taken?

bestehen aus (a, a): Das Parlament besteht aus zwei Kammern.

to consist of: The parliament consists of two chambers.

bestens = sehr gut, ausgezeichnet

optimal = very good, excellent

bestimmen: Das Grundgesetz bestimmt, daß ... . Der Bundeskanzler bestimmt die Richtlinien der Politik.

to define, to determine: The Basic Law defines that ... . The Federal Chancellor determines the guiding lines of the policies.

beweisen A (ie, ie): Mit dieser Maßnahme will man beweisen, wie fortschrittlich wir sind.

to prove: This measure is supposed to illustrate how progressive we are.

bewirken A: Was will man mit dieser Maßnahme bewirken?

to bring about: What is this measure intended to bring about?

sich ein Bild machen von: Können Sie sich ein Bild von den Schwierigkeiten machen? (= Können Sie sich die Schwierigkeiten vorstellen?)

to picture: Can you picture the difficulties? (= Can you imagine the difficulties?)

die Bundesbahn, -en

the Federal Railroad

die Bundeshauptstadt

the Federal Capital

der Bundeskanzler, —

the Federal Chancellor

das Bundesland, ¨er: Die Bundesrepublik Deutschland besteht aus zehn Bundesländern.

the Federal State: The Federal Republic of Germany consists of ten Federal States.

der Bundespräsident, -en

the Federal President

der Bundesrat

the Federal Council (upper chamber of parliament)

die Bundesregierung, -en

the Federal Government

der Bundestag

the Federal Diet (lower house of parliament)

der Bundestagsabgeordnete, -n

the Member of the Federal Diet

der Bundestagspräsident, -en

the President of the Federal Diet

der Bürger, —

the citizen

der Bursche, -n: ein junger Bursche

the lad: a young lad

die Buße, -n: Was für eine Buße hat dir der Pfarrer auferlegt?

the penance: What penance did the priest impose on you?

der Chef, -s

the director, the boss

im Dauerlauf (hier: sehr schnell; in Eile)
demokratisch: ein demokratischer Staat

diskutieren mit: Wir haben mit einem
  Bundestagsabgeordneten diskutiert.
donnern: donnernder Beifall
drücken A: Wenn Sie den Apparat ein-
  schalten müssen Sie hier den Knopf
  drücken.
durchgehend: ein durchgehendes Programm
der Ehepartner, —
sich **einig** sein über: Wir sind uns über die
  neuen Pläne einig.
sich **ein/setzen** für: Die Abgeordneten wollen sich für das neue Gesetz einsetzen.
die Einwohnerzahl, -en
ein/ziehen (o, o): Frau Neumeister ist als
  Abgeordnete in den neuen Bundestag
  eingezogen.
das **Elternhaus:** Er kommt aus einem guten Elternhaus.
enden: Als sie (mit ihrer Rede) geendet
  hatte, bekam sie begeisterten Applaus.

endgültig: das endgültige Wahlergebnis
die Erfahrung, -en: eine neue Erfahrung
die Erfolgsfrau (= eine Frau, die im öffentlichen Leben Erfolg hat)
erreichen A: Sie hat in ihrem Leben schon
  viel erreicht.
die Erziehung: die Erziehung der Kinder

die Fahne, -n: die Fahne der Bundesrepublik Deutschland
fallen (er fällt, ie, a): In den ersten Spiel-
  minuten fiel schon das erste Tor.
falten A: Falten Sie den Zettel!
fernlenken (hier: etwas von außerhalb regeln, organisieren)
föderativ: ein föderativer Staat
der Fortschritt, -e
fortschrittlich: eine fortschrittliche Partei
sich **fort/setzen:** Viele Ansichten setzen
  sich von Generation zu Generation fort.
führen: Der Abgeordnete hat mit uns ein
  längeres Gespräch geführt.
die Fußballweltmeisterschaft, -en
geheim: in geheimer Wahl

in a race (here: very fast; in a hurry)
demicratic, democratically: in a democratic state
to **discuss** with: We had a discussion with
  a Member of the Federal Diet.
to thunder: thundering applause
to **press, to push:** You have to push the
  button in order to start the machine.

continuous: a continuing program

the spouse
to **agree about:** We agree about the new
  plans.
to **stand up for:** The members are going
  to push for the new law.
the total population
to **enter:** Mrs. Neumeister entered the new
  Federal Diet as a Delegate.

the **family, the home:** He comes from a
  good home.
to **finish:** When she had finished (with her
  speech), she received enthusiastic applause.
final: the final result of the election
the experience: a new experience
the successful woman (= a woman who is
  successful in public life)
to **accomplish:** She has already accom-
  plished much in her life.
the education: the education of the
  children
the flag: the Flag of the Federal Republic
  of Germany
to **fall:** The first goal was scored in the
  very first moments of the game.
to **fold:** Fold your paper!
to run from a distance (here: to organize
  something from outside)
federal: a federal state
the progress
progressive(ly): a progressive party
to **be passed on:** Many views are passed on
  from generation to generation.
to **lead:** The Delegate held quite a long conversation with us.
the Soccer World Cup
secret(ly): a secret election

gefaßt sein auf: Wir sind auf das Schlimmste gefaßt.

gehen: Wenn es nach mir ginge, würde ich das nicht tun.

die Generation, -en

der Gesetzesvorschlag, ⁀e

gesetzgebend: die gesetzgebende Versammlung

gewinnen (a, o); Unsere Partei hat in der letzten Wahl viele Stimmen gewonnen.

glanzvoll: eine glanzvolle Feier

groß: Bei uns wird Arbeit groß geschrieben. (= Bei uns ist die Arbeit wichtig.)

das Grundgesetz, -e

grundsätzlich: meine grundsätzliche Meinung

das Hauptanliegen, —: das Hauptanliegen der Politiker

die Hauptstadt, ⁀e

die Hausfrau, -en

der **Haushalt,** -e: Meine Frau führt den Haushalt.

sich **zu helfen** wissen: Man muß sich im Leben zu helfen wissen.

sich **hin/geben** D: Geben Sie sich keinen Illusionen hin. Es bleibt alles, wie es ist.

der **Hut,** ⁀e: (figurativ) Die Abgeordnete muß Haushalt, Beruf und ihre politische Arbeit unter einen Hut bringen. (= Sie muß das alles miteinander vereinigen.)

die Illusion, -en

indem: Man wählt, indem man dem Kandidaten seiner Wahl die Stimme gibt.

der Interessenvertreter, —

das Interview, -s

der Kandidat, -en (bei einer Wahl)

knapp: knappe Zeit

die Kommunalpolitik

kurz nach 3 Uhr

das **Lampenfieber,** —: Vor einer Rede hat er immer Lampenfieber.

das Länderparlament, -e (= der Landtag, -e)

der Landtag, -e

das Lebensjahr, -e: ab dem 18. Lebensjahr

die Legislaturperiode, -n

to **be prepared for:** We are prepared for the worst.

to **go:** If it were my decision, I wouldn't do it.

the generation

the legislative proposal

legislative: the legislative body

to **win:** Our party won many votes in the last election.

splendid(ly): a splendid celebration

large: In our circles work is written in capital letters. (= Work is important in our circles.)

the Basic Law

basic, basically: my fundamental opinion

the main concern: the main concern of the politicians

the capital

the housewife

the **household:** My wife runs the household.

to **know how to take care of o. s.:** One must know how to take care of oneself in life.

to **indulge o. s.:** Don't indulge yourself in illusions. Everything's going to stay as it is.

the **hat:** (figuratively) The delegate has to reconcile household, profession and her political work. (= She has to combine it all.)

the illusion

in that, by: You vote by giving the candidate of your choice your vote.

the representative of an interest group

the interview

the candidate (in an election)

scarce: little time

the municipal politics

a little after 3 o'clock

the **stage-fright:** He always has stage-fright before a speech.

the State Parliament (= the State Diet)

the State Diet

the year (of life): after 18 years of age

the legislative term

leiten A: Wer leitet die Diskussion?

to **conduct**: Who is conducting the discussion?

die Männergesellschaft (= das Patriarchat)

the male society (= the patriarchy)

meistern A: Du wirst das Leben schon meistern.

to **master**: You're going to be able to deal with life.

das Ministeramt, ⸚er

the office of the minister

der Ministerpräsident, -en

the Minister-President, the Governor

das **Mitglied**, -er: Sie ist Mitglied des Bundestags (MdB).

the **member**: She is a Member of the Federal Diet.

mitten: mitten in einer Sitzung

in the middle of: in the middle of a session

möglich: Ich werde mein Möglichstes tun.

possible: I'll do everything possible.

mühsam = schwerfällig

laborious(ly) = heavy, heavily

nahe kommen D: Die Hochrechnung kommt dem endgültigen Ergebnis sehr nahe.

to **approximate, to come close**: The final inofficial count comes very close to the final result.

die Netzkarte, -n (= eine Fahrkarte für alle Strecken und für einen bestimmten Zeitraum)

the area ticket (= a ticket for all lines and for a certain time period)

neugewählt: der neugewählte Bundestag

newly elected: the newly elected Federal Diet

die Neuwahl, -en

the new election

die Not: mit knapper Not = im letzten Moment

the emergency: barely = at the last moment

notfalls = wenn es nötig ist

in case of emergency = if necessary

offen/stehen D (a, a): Heute stehen den Frauen viele Berufe offen.

to **be open**: Today many professions are open to women.

öffentlich: eine öffentliche Sitzung

public(ly): a public session

das **Opfer**, –: Sie kann sich nur unter Opfern politisch betätigen. Sie muß dafür viele persönliche Opfer bringen.

the **sacrifice**: She has to sacrifice to be politically active. She has to sacrifice a lot for it.

die Ovation, -en

the ovation

das Parlament, -e

the parliament

die Partei, -en

the (political) party

persönlich: ein persönliches Gespräch

personal(ly): a personal talk

der Pfarrer, –

the priest

das Plenum (= die Vollversammlung)

the plenary session (= the fully assembly)

der Politiker, –

the politician

präsent sein = anwesend sein, vorhanden sein

to be present = to be at hand

die Praxis: Theorie und Praxis

the practice: theory and practice

die Praxis, die Praxen: eine Arztpraxis

the doctor's office: a medical office

die Preisbindung, -en (= ein festgelegter, für alle gültiger Preis)

the price control (= a price controlled and applicable to all)

programmieren A: Die Mädchen werden schon von klein auf auf ihre Rolle als Hausfrau programmiert.

to **program**: Girls are programmed from early childhood for their role as housewives.

prominent: ein prominenter Politiker

prominent: a prominent politician

von rechts bis links (hier im Parlament)

from the right to the left (in parliament)

der Rechtsstaat, -en

the constitutional state

eine **Rede** halten: Wer hält heute im Parlament eine Rede?

to **give a speech:** Who is holding a speech in Parliament today?

die Richtlinie, -n: die Richtlinien der Politik

the guideline: the guidelines of politics

die Rolle, -n: die Rolle als Ehefrau und Mutter

the role: the role as wife and mother

schießen A (o, o): Wer hat das erste Tor geschossen?

to **shoot:** Who scored the first goal?

schwarz-rot-gold: Die Fahne der Bundesrepublik ist schwarz-rot-gold.

black-red-gold: The flag of the Federal Republic of Germany is black, red and gold.

schwer: Mir fällt die Arbeit schwer.

difficult: This is hard work for me.

selten: äußerst selten

rare(ly): very rarely

die Sitzung, -en

the session

sozial: ein sozialer Staat

social: a social state

sprechen (er spricht, a, o): Der Erfolg spricht für sich.

to **speak:** Success speaks for itself.

das Staatsoberhaupt, ̈-er

the head of state

der Stadtpfarrer, —

the town priest

die Stimme, -n (bei einer Wahl)

the vote (in an election)

stimmen: Die Rechnung stimmt. Das stimmt, was Sie sagen.

to **be correct:** The bill is correct. What you say is correct.

die Stimmenauszählung, -en (die Stimmen aus/zählen)

the counting of the votes

der Stimmzettel, —

the ballot

die Struktur, -en

the structure

die Sünde, -n

the sin

das System, -e

the system

systematisch

systematic, systematically

das Tempo (= die Schnelligkeit)

the speed (= the velocity)

die Theorie, -n: Theorie und Praxis

the theory: theory and practice

das Tor, -e (beim Fußballspiel): ein Tor schießen

the goal (in a soccer game): to score a goal

typisch

typical(ly)

überall

everywhere, all over

überlegen: Überlege nicht so lange!

to **contemplate:** Don't think so long!

der Umschlag, ̈-e: der Briefumschlag, ̈-e

the envelope: the envelope for a letter

ungeduldig

impatient(ly)

unmittelbar

immediate(ly)

unterbrechen A (er unterbricht, a, o): Das Programm wird für zehn Minuten unterbrochen.

to **interrupt:** The program will be interrupted for ten minutes.

unterrepräsentiert sein: Die Frauen sind im Parlament unterrepräsentiert.

to **be underrepresented:** Women are underrepresented in parliament.

die Veranstaltung, -en

the event

auf sich **vereinigen** A: Unsere Partei hat die meisten Stimmen auf sich vereinigt.

to **unite:** Our party received most of the votes.

die Versammlung, -en

the meeting

das **Vertrauen** schenken D: Welchem Kandidaten können wir unser Vertrauen schenken?

die Vertretung, -en

die Volksvertretung

vor/kochen A: Frau Neumeister will das Essen für morgen vorkochen.

vor/liegen (a, e): Liegen irgendwelche neuen Nachrichten vor?

Vorrang haben: Welche Maßnahmen haben Vorrang?

vor/schlagen A (er schlägt vor, u, a): Wer ist als Kandidat unserer Partei vorgeschlagen worden?

vor/setzen A: Sage mir bitte, was wir unseren Gästen vorsetzen sollen!

das Vorurteil, -e: falsche Vorurteile

wahlberechtigt: Mit 18 Jahren ist jeder Bürger wahlberechtigt.

das Wahlergebnis, -se

die Wählerstimme, -n

der Wahlkreis, -e

das Wahllokal, -e

die Wahlurne, -n

die Wahlveranstaltung, -en

die Wahlversammlung, -en

waldreich: waldreiche Gebiete

weiblich: die weiblichen Abgeordneten

die Welt

werfen A (er wirft, a, o): Werfen Sie den Brief in den Briefkasten!

wildern: Der Bursche hat hier im Wald gewildert.

die Wirklichkeit: in Wirklichkeit

der **Wohnsitz, -e:** Wo ist Ihr Wohnsitz?

der Zahnarzt, ̈-e

die Zeit: zur Zeit

zumute sein: Wie ist Ihnen jetzt zumute?

zunächst = zuerst

zurecht/kommen (a, o): Ich bin zur Sitzung zurechtgekommen.

die Zusammensetzung: die Zusammensetzung des Parlaments

zusammen/stellen A: Der neue Bundeskanzler muß jetzt seine Regierung zusammenstellen.

zusammen/treten (er tritt zusammen, a, e): Heute tritt der neue Bundestag zusammen.

to **place trust:** In which candidate can we place our trust?

the representation

the representation of the people

to **cook in advance:** Mrs. Neumeister wants to cook dinner in advance for tomorrow.

to **be present:** Is there any news?

to **have priority:** Which measures have priority?

to **propose:** Who has been proposed as the candidate of our party?

to **serve:** Please tell me what we should serve to our guests!

the prejudice: false prejudices

eligible to vote: Every citizen who is 18 years of age is eligible to vote.

the election results

the vote

the election district

the polling center

the ballot box

the election meeting, the election event

the election meeting

well-wooded: well-wooded areas

female: the women delegates

the world

to **throw:** Throw the letter into the mail box!

to **poach:** The lad has poached here in the forest.

the reality: in reality

the **place of residence:** Where do you live?

the dentist

the time: at the present time

to **feel:** How do you feel now?

primarily = first

to **come just in time:** I arrived just in time for the session.

the composition: the composition of parliament

to **put together, to form:** The new Federal Chancellor has to form his government now.

to **assemble:** The new Federal Diet is assembling today.

der Abschluß der Ausbildung
die Akte, -n
allmählich: Deine Fragen werden allmählich lästig.
anscheinend (= wie es scheint): Er hilft anscheinend unserem Kollegen.
auf/bauen A: Er hat die Akten um sich herum (auf dem Schreibtisch) aufgebaut.
auf/treten (er tritt auf, a, e): (hier: komken)
die Ausbildung
die Ausbildungszeit, -en
ausgesprochen: Das Zimmer ist ausgesprochen häßlich.
aus/graben A (er gräbt aus, u, a): (figurativ) Ich bin dabei, meine verschütteten Englischkenntnisse wieder auszugraben.
aus/leihen A (ie, ie): Wo kann ich hier Bücher ausleihen?
aus/reichen: Meine finanziellen Mittel reichen für ein Studium nicht aus.
aus/stehen können A: Ich kann diesen Menschen nicht ausstehen. (= Ich kann diesen Menschen nicht leiden.)
der Auszubildende, -n: jemand, der ausgebildet wird
beheben A (o, o): Der Mechaniker versuchte, die Panne zu beheben.
benutzen A: Wer hat meine Schreibmaschine benutzt?
die Benutzung
ein **Berg** von Akten: Ich sitze den ganzen Tag hinter einem Berg von Akten.
beschreiben A (ie, ie): Können Sie den Mann beschreiben, dem Sie gestern hier begegnet sind?
beschwindeln A: Mein Sohn hat mich beschwindelt.
der Betrag, ⁻e
der Bewohner, −: die Bewohner eines Hauses
die Bude, -n: (salopp für:) ein kleines Zimmer
da und dort: Ich leihe mir da und dort Bücher aus.
das **Darlehen,** −: Der Staat gibt den Studenten zinslose Darlehen.

the completion of one's education
the file
gradual(ly): Gradually your questions are getting bothersome.
apparent(ly): (= as it seems) Apparently he's helping our colleague.
to **build, to construct:** He piled up his files around himself (on the desk).

to appear (here: to come)

the education, the training
the time of education, or training
decided(ly): The room is decidedly ugly.

to **dig up, or out:** (figuratively) I'm in the process of digging out my buried knowledge of English.
to **borrow:** Where can I borrow books here?
to **suffice:** My financial means don't suffice for academic studies.
to **be able to stand:** I can't stand this person. (= I don't like this person.)

the trainee: someone who is being trained

to **eliminate, to take care of:** The mechanic tried to deal with the break-down.
to **use:** Who used my typewriter?

the use
a **pile,** or **mountain, of papers:** I sit here all day behind a mountain of papers.
to **describe:** Can you describe the man who you met here yesterday?

to **cheat, to swindle:** My son cheated me.

the sum, the amount
the occupant, the tenant: the occupants of a house
the hole in the wall: (everyday language for:) a small room
here and there: I borrow books here and there.
the **loan:** The government gives students loans without interest.

die Dauer der Ausbildung
derzeit: Mein Mann arbeitet derzeit im Rathaus.
das Ding, -e: die Dinge des täglichen Lebens
ehrlich: ein ehrlicher Mensch
eigentlich: Wer ist eigentlich dieser junge Mann? — Eigentlich müßte ich das wissen.
die Eignung, -en: die Eignung zum Politiker
das Einstellungsgespräch, -e: das Gespräch, das ein Chef mit jemandem führt, der in die Firma eingestellt werden möchte
das Elternhaus: Der junge Mann stammt aus einem guten Elternhaus.
endlos: eine endlose Diskussion
die Englischkenntnisse (Plural)
entlarven A: Der Mann wurde als Dieb entlarvt.
sich entscheiden für: Haben Sie sich schon für einen bestimmten Beruf entschieden?
entsprechen D (er entspricht, a, o): Die Ausbildung meines Sohnes entspricht seinen Neigungen.
ernsthaft: ein ernsthafter Mensch, eine ernsthafte Arbeit
F.D.P. = Freie Demokratische Partei
finanziell: die finanzielle Unterstützung
die Förderung, -en: die Förderung junger Menschen bei ihrer Ausbildung
der Förderungsbetrag, ‥e: der Geldbetrag, der zur Förderung von Auszubildenden ausgezahlt wird
die Fortsetzung, -en: die Fortsetzung des Studiums
fragen nach: Heute hat jemand nach Ihnen gefragt.
der Frager, —: jemand, der Fragen stellt
die Fraktion, -en (im Parlament)
gesichert: eine finanziell gesicherte Ausbildung
geschäftig: geschäftige Leute
gewähren D + A: Wer gewährt Ihnen die Unterstützung?
das Gewissen: Er hat ein schlechtes Gewissen.

the time period of education, or training
at present: At present my husband works in the City Hall.
the thing: the little matters of everyday life
honest: an honest person
really, actually: Who is this youn man really? — Actually, I should know.
the qualification: the qualification to be a politician
the employment interview: the discussion which a director has with someone who wants to be employed by the company
the family, the home: The young man comes from a good home.
endless(ly): an endless discussion
the knowledge of the English language
to unmask: The man was unmasked as a thief.
to decide in favor of: Have you decided on your profession already?
to suit: My son's training suits his inclinations.
serious(ly): a serious person, serious work
Free Democratic Party
financial(ly): the financial support
the help, the support, the encouragement: the supporting of young people during their education, or training
the sum of financial assistance: the amount of money paid for the support of students or trainees
the continuation: the continuation of studies
to ask for: Today somebody inquired about you.
the inquirer: somebody who asks questions
the parliamentary party
secured: a financially secured education
officious(ly): officious people
to grant: Who's granting you the aid?
the conscience: He has a bad conscience.

die **Gunst:** Er arbeitet nur zu seinen Gunsten.

the **favor:** He only works for his own benefit.

hegen A: Er hegt gegen jedermann Mißtrauen.

to **harbor:** He harbors suspicion against everyone.

helfen: Er weiß sich zu helfen.

to **help:** He knows how to help himself.

hell: ein helles Zimmer

light: a light room

häßlich: ein häßlicher Mensch, ein häßliches Zimmer

ugly: an ugly person, an ugly room

die **Hilfe:** Wir sind dem Verletzten zu Hilfe gekommen.

the **help, the aid:** We aided the injured person.

die Höhe: die Höhe des Geldbetrags

the amount: the amount of money

irgendwann: Ich werde dir irgendwann einmal schreiben.

sometime or other: I'll write you sometime or other.

je nach Frage: je nachdem, wie gefragt wurde

according to the question: according to how he was asked

jedermann: Er ist zu jedermann freundlich.

everyone: He is friendly to everyone.

das Jugendreferat, -e

the Department of Juvenile Welfare

der Jugendschutz

the protection of youth

die Kenntnisse (Plural)

the knowledge

das Kleid, -er

the dress

komisch: eine komische Frage

strange: a strange question

kommen (a, o): Wie kommt man am schnellsten zu Geld?

to **come:** What's the quickest way to get rich?

lästig: lästige Fragen

annoying: annoying questions

das Leben

the life

leer/stehen (a, a): Das Zimmer steht leer.

to **be empty:** The room is empty.

die Leistung, -en: gute Leistungen in der Schule

the achievement: good achievements in school

lösen A: Wir haben endlich das Problem gelöst.

to **solve:** We finally solved the problem.

die Lüge, -n

the lie

die Medizin: ein Student der Medizin (stud. med.)

the medicine: a medical student

merkwürdig: ein merkwürdiger Mensch, eine merkwürdige Frage

strange, unusual: a strange person, a strange question

das Mißtrauen

the suspicion

das Mittel, —: finanzielle Mittel

the means: financial means

möglicherweise

possibly

monatlich: die monatliche Miete

monthly: the monthly rent

moralisch

moral(ly)

das Motiv, -e

the motive

die **Mühe, -n:** Wir hatten Mühe, den Mann zu verstehen.

the **trouble:** We had trouble understanding the man.

die **Nase, -n:** Der Zug ist uns vor der Nase weggefahren.

the **nose:** The train left just as we got there.

die Neigung, -en: künstlerische Neigungen

the inclination: artistic inclinations

die Ordnung: Das hat seine Ordnung!

the order: That is in order!

die **Panne, -n:** Unterwegs hatten wir mit unserem Wagen eine Panne.

the **break-down:** On the road we had a break-down with our car.

der Personalchef, -s

the director of personnel

das **Pferd, -e:** Unser neuer Kollege arbeitet wie ein Pferd.

the **horse:** Our new colleague works like a horse.

der Praktikant, -en

the trainee in a profession

die Rate, -n

the installment

das Rathaus, ‒er

the city hall

der Rathausgang, ‒e = Korridor im Rathaus

the city hall corridor

der Raum, ‒e

the room

räumen A: Wir müssen heute unser Zimmer räumen. (= Wir müssen heute unser Zimmer frei machen.)

to **move out, to clear:** Today we have to move out of our room. (= Today we have to clear our room.)

der **Rechtsanspruch, ‒e:** Die jungen Leute haben einen Rechtsanspruch auf Ausbildungsförderung.

the **legal claim:** The young people have a legal claim to aid for their education.

das Ressort, -s

the department

das Resultat, -e

the result

sich **richten** nach: Die Höhe des Förderungsbetrags richtet sich nach den persönlichen Verhältnissen des Auszubildenden.

to **depend on:** The amount of the aid depends on the personal circumstances of the trainee.

schmeicheln D: Er schmeichelt dem Chef.

to **flatter:** He flatters his boss.

der Schreibtisch, -e

the desk

schriftlich wiedergeben: Können Sie das schriftlich wiedergeben, was er Ihnen gesagt hat?

to **put in writing:** Can you put what he told you in writing?

schwindeln: Der Junge hat geschwindelt.

to **cheat, to swindle:** The boy cheated.

die Senatskanzlei, -en

the Chancellery of the Senate

das Sitzungszimmer, —

the committee room

der Soziologe, -n

the sociologist

Die SPD-Fraktion: die Fraktion der Sozialdemokratischen Partei Deutschlands

the SPD Parliamentary Party: the Parliamentary Party of the German Social Democratic Party

der Staat, -en

the state

still: Er arbeitet still in seinem Zimmer.

quiet(ly): He works quietly in his room.

der Stolz: voller Stolz

the pride: proud(ly)

die Studie, -n: eine Studie über die heutigen Jugendprobleme

the study: a study about contemporary juvenile problems

das **Studium, die Studien:** Er betreibt Studien über Sozialfragen.

the **study:** He conducts studies about social questions.

stützen A: Die Wissenschaft stützt unsere Theorien.

to **support:** Science supports our theories.

die Tischlampe, -n

the desk lamp

der Umstand, ‒e: unter Umständen

the circumstance: under certain circumstances

unauffällig (= ohne aufzufallen): Er ging unauffällig aus dem Zimmer.

inconspicuous(ly) (= without being noticed): He left the room inconspicuously.

unbefugt: Für Unbefugte verboten!

unauthorized: Authorized persons only!

ungewohnt: ungewohnte Arbeit

unaccustomed: unaccustomed work

unsympathisch

disagreeable

die Unterstützung, -en: finanzielle Unterstützung

the support, the aid: financial support

die Verhältnisse (Plural): persönliche Verhältnisse

the circumstances: personal circumstances

sich **verlaufen** (er verläuft sich, ie, au): Ich habe mich in der Stadt verlaufen.

to **get lost:** I got lost in the city.

verschüttete Kenntnisse (= Kenntnisse, die man früher gehabt hat, die man aber nicht mehr gegenwärtig hat)

buried knowledge (= knowledge which one had at an earlier date, but which is no longer at hand)

völlig = vollkommen

complete(ly) = perfect(ly)

sich **vorbereiten** auf A: Er bereitete sich auf seine Prüfung vor.

to **prepare o. s.:** He prepared himself for his examination.

vor/führen A: Das Mannequin führt neue Kleider vor.

to **present:** The fashion model presents new dresses.

vor/haben: Was haben Sie für heute vor?

to **plan, to intend:** What are your plans for today?

sich **vor/stellen:** Ich werde mich heute meinem neuen Chef vorstellen.

to **introduce o. s.:** I'm going to introduce myself to my new boss today.

die Wahrheit

the truth

der **Weg:** Er macht sich auf den Weg ins Rathaus.

the **way:** He sets out for City Hall.

weiblich: weibliche Angestellte

female, feminine: women employees

wieder/geben A (er gibt wieder, a, e): Haben Sie das auch genau wiedergegeben, was Ihnen der Chef gesagt hat?

to **report:** Have you reported exactly what the boss said to you?

ziehen (o, o): Wir ziehen heute in ein anderes Zimmer.

to **move:** Today we're moving into another room.

zinslos: ein zinsloses Darlehen

without interest: a loan without interest

zufällig

by accident

zu/schießen A (o, o): Der Staat schießt zum Studium Geld zu.

to **contribute:** The state contributes money for academic studies.

Abschnitt 12

das Ackerland

the arable land

ab/trennen A: Die Membrane trennt die Salze und Schadstoffe des Meerwassers ab.

to **separate:** The membrane separates the salts and harmful substances from the sea water.

allein = nur

alone = only

die Arbeitsweise, -n: die Arbeitsweise eines Computers

the manner, or mode, of operation: the mode of operation of a computer

auf/brechen A (er bricht auf, a, o): Er hat ein Auto aufgebrochen.

to **break, or force, open:** He broke into a car.

auf/geben A (er gibt auf, a, e): Er gab die Bemühungen auf.

to **give up:** He gave up the efforts.

aus/bauen A: Er hat den Motor aus dem Wagen ausgebaut.

to **remove:** He removed the motor from the car.

die Auszahlung, -en

the payment

aus/bezahlen A: Wann wird das Geld aus-bezahlt?
to **pay out:** When is the money going to be paid?

aus/werfen A (er wirft aus, a, o): Der Computer wirft die Zahlen aus.
to **throw out:** The computer puts out the numbers.

die Bank, -en
the bank

der Bankauszug, ̈-e
the bank statement

die Bankspesen (Plural)
the bank charges

bedauern A: Wir bedauern den Fehler, den wir gemacht haben.
to **regret:** We regret the mistake that we made.

bedienen A: Können Sie die Maschine bedienen?
to **operate:** Can you operate the machine?

belasten A: Wir haben Ihr Konto mit 100 Mark belastet.
to **charge:** We've charged 100 DM to your account.

das Benzin
the gasoline

beruhigen A: Das hat mich beruhigt.
to **calm down:** That calmed me down.

in **Berührung** kommen mit: Täglich kommen wir mit Dingen in Berührung, die aus Erdöl hergestellt sind.
to **come into contact with:** Every day we come into contact with things which are made from petroleum.

bestätigen A: Wir bestätigen den Empfang Ihres Briefes vom 5.3.78.
to **confirm:** We confirm the reception of your letter from March 5, 1978.

der Betrag, ̈-e
the amount

die Beute
the booty

bekämpfen A: Die Schädlinge müssen bekämpft werden.
to **fight:** Vermin and parasites must be fought.

bleiben (ie, ie): Was bleibt uns noch, wenn wir kein Erdöl mehr haben?
to **remain:** What are we going to do when we have no more petroleum?

die Botschaft der Bundesrepublik Deutschland
the Embassy of the Federal Republic of Germany

die Buchung, -en
the entry (into an account)

die Buchungsgebühr, -en
the entry fee

der Buchungsvorgang, ̈-e
the entry process

die Bürokratie, -n
the bureaucracy

bürokratisch
bureaucratic

bewässern A: Das Land wird bewässert.
to **irrigate:** The land is being irrigated.

der Computer, —
the computer

die Datenverarbeitungsanlage, -n
the data processing equipment

der **Dienst, -e:** Der Mann hat uns seine Dienste angeboten.
the **service:** The man offered us his services.

das Ding, -e: die schönen Dinge des Lebens
the thing: the nice things of life

der Dünger, —
the manure

EDV = Elektronische Datenverarbeitung
electronic data processing

das Eiweiß
the protein

der Empfang Ihres Schreibens v. 5.3.78
the reception of your letter from 3.5.78

entfernen A (hier: weg/bringen)
to remove (here: to take away)

entstehen (a, a):Wieviel Kosten sind bei dem Projekt entstanden?
to **arise:** What costs arose in this project?

die Enttäuschung, -en: zur Enttäuschung der Leute
the disappointment: to the disappointment of the people

die Erde = die Welt
the earth = the world

das Erdöl
erfolgen: Die Abrechnung erfolgt über EDV.
ergreifen A (i, i): Die Diebe ergriffen die Flucht.
der Ernteertrag, ⍩e
die Erschöpfung: vor Erschöpfung
ersetzen A: Wer soll den Schaden ersetzen?
ertappen A: Der Polizist ertappte den Mann beim Diebstahl.
die Flucht ergreifen: Hat der Dieb die Flucht ergriffen?
folgern: Was folgern Sie aus der Sache?

fordern A: Er forderte Geld von mir.

fördern A: In der Nordsee wird Öl gefördert.
die Forschung, -en
die Frage: eine Frage der Zeit
in Gang setzen A: Jetzt wird die Maschine in Gang gesetzt.
die Gebührenabrechnung, -en
der Gegenwert
der Geldeingang, ⍩e (auf ein Konto)
die Genauigkeit
gering: ein geringer Betrag
geringfügig: eine geringfügige Gutschrift, ein geringfügiger Fehler
die Girozentrale, -n
gleichgültig = egal
gut/schreiben D; A (ie, ie): Wir haben Ihnen den Betrag von DM 100,— gutgeschrieben.
die Gutschrift, -en: eine Gutschrift über DM 100,—
die Hälfte, -n
das Heizöl
sich heraus/stellen: Bei der Jahresabrechnung hat sich ein Fehler herausgestellt.
her/stellen A: Man versucht, aus Meerwasser Trinkwasser herzustellen.
hervor/gehen aus (i, a): Wie aus meinem Bankauszug hervorgeht, ...
hiermit = mit diesem Brief
hinzu/kommen (a, o): Zum Rechnungsbetrag kommen noch die Kosten für Porto und Verpackung hinzu.
das Huhn, ⍩er

the petroleum
to **take place** (here): The account is settled by electronic data processing.
to **take hold of:** The thieves took to flight.
the yield, the harvest
the exhaustion: from exhaustion
to **substitute:** Who's going to pay for the damage?
to **catch, to surprise:** The policeman caught the thief in the act.
to **take to flight:** Did the thief run away?
to **draw conclusions:** What do you conclude from this matter?
to **demand:** He demanded money from me.
to **raise:** Oil is being pumped from the North Sea.
the research
the question: a question of time
to **set in motion:** Now the machine is being set in motion.
the settling of the charges
the equivalent
the deposit of money (into an account)
the accuracy
small: a small amount
insignificant: an insignificant credit, an insignificant mistake
the center for bank endorsements
indifferent = the same
to **credit:** We credited you with the sum of 100 DM.
the credit: a credit of 100 DM
the half
the heating oil
to **become evident, to appear:** A mistake appeared on the annual balance sheet.
to **produce:** The attempt is being made to produce drinking water from sea water.
to **proceed from:** As my bank account shows, ...
with this = with this letter
to **be added to:** The costs for postage and handling are being added to the sum total of the amount.
the hen

die **Höhe:** Der Betrag wird Ihnen in voller Höhe ersetzt.

the **total:** You will be credited with the total amount

der **Hunger:** Zunächst müssen die Kinder ihren Hunger stillen.

the **hunger:** First the children have to appease their hunger.

die Industrie, -n

the industry

investieren A: Wir wollen noch mehr Geld in die Firma investieren.

to **invest:** We want to invest even more money in the business.

irrtümlich

erroneous(ly)

die Jahresabrechnung, -en

the annual balance sheet

der Jahresausgleich (bei der Kontoführung)

the balance of the year's account

die Kasse, -n

the cash register

der Kontoauszug, "-e

the bank statement

die **Kosten** (Plural): Wieviel Kosten sind Ihnen bei dem Geschäft entstanden?

the **costs:** What expenditures arose for you in this transaction?

die **Lage:** Wir sind nicht in der Lage, mehr Geld zu investieren.

the **position:** We're not in the position to invest more money.

laut D: laut Jahresabrechnung

according to: according to the annual balance sheet

die Lokalredaktion, -en

the editing office for local news

das Meerwasser

the sea water

menschlich: wie ein Mensch

human(ly): like a human being

die Membrane, -n

the membrane

die Milliarde, -n = tausend Millionen

the billion = a thousand million

die Mineralölindustrie, -n

the petroleum industry

mit/teilen D + A: Wie Sie mir in Ihrem Brief mitteilten, ...

to **inform:** As you informed me in your letter ...

die Motorhaube, -n

the hood

der Motorraum (im Auto)

the engine space (in a car)

die Muskelkraft, "-e

the muscular strength

nach/prüfen A: Bitte prüfen Sie die Rechnung nach!

to **check:** Please check the bill!

die Nahrung

the food, the nourishment

zur **Neige** gehen: Die Ölreserven gehen langsam zur Neige.

to **come to an end:** The oil reserves are slowly coming to an end.

der Ozean, -e

the ocean

die Pflanzenkrankheit, -en

the herbivorous disease

die Portoauslage, -n = die Kosten für Porto

the costs for postage

pro Buchung = für jede Buchung

per entry = for each entry

der Rechner, — = der Computer, —

the computer

reden: gar nicht davon zu reden (= ich will gar nicht erst erwähnen, ...)

to talk: not to mention it at all (= I don't even want to mention ...)

reklamieren A: Er hat das Geld reklamiert.

to **reclaim, to request a refund:** He requested a refund of the money.

die Rückvergütung, -en

the reimbursement

sagen: sage und schreibe = tatsächlich

to say: really = in fact

das Salz, -e

the salt

der Schädling, -e (Insekten usw.)

the vermin, the parasite (insects, etc.)

der Schadstoff, -e

the harmful substance

schieben A (o, o): Wir müssen den Wagen schieben.

to **push:** We have to push the car.

das Schreiben, — = der Brief, -e — the letter

der Schuppen, — — the shed

das Schwein, -e — the pig

sichern A: Die Ernteerträge müssen auch in den nächsten Jahren gesichert sein. — to **secure:** The harvest yields for the coming years also have to be assured.

der Spott — the ridicule

stellen A: Die Polizei hat die Autodiebe gestellt. — to **catch:** The police caught the car thieves.

der Steuerberater, — — the tax accountant

stillen A: Wir stillen zuerst unseren Hunger. — to **satisfy:** We appease our hunger first.

die Stromrechnung, -en — the electric bill

die Täuschung, -en — the deception, the fraud

trauen D: Ich traute meinen Augen nicht, als ich das sah. — to **trust:** I didn't believe my eyes when I saw that.

das Trinkwasser — the drinking water

überprüfen A: Wir müssen die Rechnung zuerst überprüfen. — to **check:** First we have to check the bill.

überzahlt: der überzahlte Betrag = der zuviel bezahlte Betrag — overpaid: the amount overpaid = the amount paid in excess

das Unkraut, ⁻er — the weed

verbessern A: Im letzten Jahr sind die Ernteerträge verbessert worden. — to **improve:** Last year the harvest yields increased.

verfüttern A an A: Was kann man an Hühner verfüttern? — to **feed:** What can chickens be fed?

vergeblich: Ich habe vergeblich versucht, den Chef zu erreichen. — in **vain:** I tried in vain to reach the director.

verhüten A: Wie kann man Schaden verhüten? — to **prevent:** How can damage be prevented?

vermeiden (ie, ie): Es läßt sich nicht vermeiden, daß ... — to **avoid:** It is impossible to avoid ...

vermutlich — supposed(ly)

verrechnen A: Verrechnen Sie bitte den überzahlten Betrag mit der nächsten Rechnung! — to **charge, to settle:** Please adjust the overpaid amount in the next bill.

verschenken A: Er hat das Geld, das er gewonnen hat, wieder verschenkt. — to **give away:** He gave away the money that he won.

das Versorgungsgebiet des Elektrizitätswerks = das Gebiet, das das Elektrizitätswerk (mit Strom) versorgt — the supply area of the electrical utility company = the area which the utility company supplies (with electricity)

das **Verständnis:** Ich bitte Sie dafür um Verständnis, daß ... — the **understanding:** I ask your understanding for the fact that ...

verstecken A: Die Diebe haben ihre Beute versteckt. — to **hide:** The thieves hid their booty.

versuchen A: Sie haben versucht, die Flucht zu ergreifen. — to **try:** They tried to run away.

vertilgen A: Womit kann man Unkraut vertilen? — to **destroy:** How can weeds be destroyed?

die Verwaltung, -en — the administration

verwunderlich: Das ist nicht verwunderlich. = Man braucht sich nicht darüber zu wundern.

verzichten auf A: Ich verzichte auf die Rückvergütung des überzahlten Betrags.

der Vorgang, ⸗e

vor/kommen (a, o): In der Jahresabrechnung dürfen keine Fehler vorkommen.

die Wasserreserve, -n

weiter/reichen A: Wir haben Ihren Brief an das E-Werk weitergereicht.

weiter/verarbeiten A: Hier wird das Erdöl weiterverarbeitet.

der Wert: Wenn Sie darauf wertlegen, zahlen wir Ihnen das Geld sofort aus.

das Ziel, -e

zu/gehen D + A (i, a): Heute ist uns eine Gutschrift zugegangen.

die Zukunft: in Zukunft

zurück/erstatten D + A: Dürfen wir Ihnen den überzahlten Betrag wieder zurückerstatten?

zurückhaltend: Der junge Mann ist sehr zurückhaltend.

astonishing: That is not astonishing. = One needn't be surprised.

to **renounce, to wave:** I wave the reimbursement of the overpaid amount.

the process

to **appear:** No errors may appear in the annual balance sheet.

the water reserves

to **forward:** We forwarded your letter to the electrical utilities company.

to **process:** The petroleum is processed here.

the value: If it is important to you, we'll pay you the money immediately.

the goal

to **reach:** Today a credit arrived.

the future: in the future

to **reimburse:** May we reimburse you for the overpaid amount?

reserved, shy: The young man is very reserved.

Abschnitt 13

der **Absatz:** Wie groß war im letzten Jahr der Absatz dieser Automobile?

ADAC = Allgemeiner Deutscher Automobil-Club

sich **an/eignen:** Wenn man sich eine fremde Sache aneignet, ist das Diebstahl.

an/fertigen A: Ich muß von der Sitzung ein Protokoll anfertigen.

der Angeklagte, -n

die Anklage (bei Gericht)

an/melden A: Ich muß meinen neuen Wagen bei der Zulassungsstelle anmelden.

die Anzeige, -n (bei der Polizei)

auf/brechen A (er bricht auf, a, o): Die Diebe haben das Auto aufgebrochen.

auf/fallen (er fällt auf, ie, a): Was fällt Ihnen hier auf? — Der Mann ist der Polizei schon einmal aufgefallen.

auf/schauen: Bei der Verhandlung schaute der Protokollführer mehrmals auf.

the **sale, the turnover:** How many of these automobiles were sold last year?

the German Automobile Association

to **appropriate, to acquire:** If one appropriates other people's property, it is theft.

to **prepare:** I have to keep the minutes of the session.

the defendant

the charge, the accusation (in court)

to **register:** I have to register my new car at the Motor Vehicle Bureau.

the report (to the police)

to **break open:** The thieves broke into the car.

to **attract attention:** What do you notice here? — The man attracted the attention of the police once before.

to **look up:** During the hearing the recorder looked up several times.

der **Aufwand:** Wie groß war der Aufwand bei der Fahndung nach den Dieben?

the **expenditure:** How much trouble did the police go through in searching for the thieves?

der Ausgang: der Ausgang des Prozesses

the result: the result of the proceedings

das Ausland

the foreign countries

aus/schreiben A: Der Verkäufer schrieb einen Kassenzettel aus.

to **write out:** The salesperson wrote out a register receipt.

das Autoklaugeschäft (hier salopp für: das Geschäft, das mit Autodiebstählen gemacht wird)

the business of auto thievery (here everyday language for: the business which is conducted around auto thievery)

die Bande, -n

the gang

bedienen: Welcher Verkäufer hat Sie bedient?

to wait on, to serve: Which salesperson waited on you?

die Behörde, -n

the (administrative) authorities

beispielsweise = zum Beispiel (z. B.)

for example

beobachten A: Ich habe den Jungen genau beobachtet.

to **observe, to watch:** I observed the boy very carefully.

bereit/stehen (a, a): Steht für mich ein Wagen bereit?

to **be ready:** Is there a car ready for me?

sich **beschaffen** A: Wir müssen uns noch die Papiere beschaffen.

to **get, to procure:** We still have to get the papers.

beschwören A: Können Sie Ihre Aussage beschwören?

to **testify an oath:** Can you swear to your statement?

der Beteiligte, -n: jemand, der an einem Prozeß (usw.) beteiligt ist

the person, or party, involved: someone who participates in legal proceedings (etc.)

beweglich: eine bewegliche Sache (Gerichtsausdruck)

movable: a movable object (court expression)

bezeichnen A als: Diese Manipulation wird als „Herzverpflanzung" bezeichnet.

to **be called:** This operation is designated as a "heart transplant".

die Branche, -n

the branch

denken von: Du denkst schlecht von mir.

to **think of:** Do you think badly of me?

das Diebesauto, -s (= das gestohlene Auto)

the stolen car

der Diebstahl, ⸚e

the theft

einfach = nur

simple, simply = only

ein/führen A: = importieren A

to introduce = to import

ein/pflanzen A

to plant into, to implant

ein/stellen A: Der Prozeß ist inzwischen eingestellt worden.

to **suspend:** Meanwhile the proceedings have been suspended.

einwandfrei: einwandfreie Papiere

faultless(ly): documents completely in order

die Elster, -n

the magpie

die Entdeckung des Diebstahls

the discovery of the theft

die Entschuldigung, -en

the excuse, the apology

der Entschuldigungsbrief, -e

the letter of apology

entwenden = stehlen

to make off with = to steal

entwertet (z. B. Fahrschein, Paß usw.)

void (for example, ticket, passport)

erheben (o, o): Gegen den Mann ist Anklage erhoben worden.

to **raise:** Charges have been raised against the man.

erlassen (er erläßt, ie, a): Ein neues Gesetz ist erlassen worden.
der Eröffnungsbeschluß (bei Gericht)
extrem schlecht
die Fachkreise (Plural) = die Experten
die Fahrgestellnummer, -n (beim Auto)
die Fahrtkosten (Plural)
der Fall, "-e: ein juristischer Fall
fälschen: gefälschtes Geld, gefälschte Dokumente
die Fertigkeit, -en: technische Fertigkeiten

fest/halten A (er hält fest, ie, a): Der Polizist hielt den Dieb fest.
fest/setzen A: Wird für die Verhandlung ein neuer Termin festgesetzt?
formulieren A: Der Staatsanwalt formuliert die Anklageschrift.
frisieren A: Es ist verboten, Motore zu frisieren.
gängig: ein gängiges Verfahren = ein übliches Verfahren
der Gegenstand: der Gegenstand der Verhandlung

gehen (i, a): Worum geht es bei der Gerichtsverhandlung? — Das Protokoll geht jetzt an die Staatsanwaltschaft.

die Gelegenheit, -en
gelegentlich
das Gericht, -e
geschehen (a, e): Der Diebstahl geschah in einem Kaufhaus.
groß: ganz groß (hier: mit viel Aufwand)
der Hausdetektiv, -e: ein Detektiv, der in einem Kaufhaus angestellt ist
die Herzverpflanzung, -en = die Herztransplantation, -en
hindern A: Der Detektiv hinderte den Jungen am Weglaufen.
hinterher: Hinterher weiß man alles besser.

die Hinterhofwerkstatt, "-e: eine kleine Werkstatt (, die im Hinterhof eines Gebäudekomplexes liegt)
die Hochkonjunktur
hundertfach: Autodiebstähle kommen hundertfach vor.
das Jugendamt, "-er
der Jugendgerichtshelfer, —
der Justizwachtmeister, —

to issue: A new law has been issued.

the decision to hold trial (in court)
extremely bad
the experts
the chassis number (in a car)
the fares
the case: a legal case
to forge, to counterfeit: counterfeit money, forged documents
the skill: technical skills

to detain: The policeman detained the thief.
to fix, to arrange: Is a new date being set for the trial?
to formulate: The public prosecutor formulates the indictment.
to trim, to alter: Altering motors is prohibited.
usual, common: a common procedure, a usual procedure
the object: the subject of the trial

to go: What is this trial all about? — Now the records go to the public prosecutor's office.
the opportunity
occasional(ly)
the court
to happen: The theft occurred in a department store.
great: very great (here: with much trouble)
the house detective: a detective, who is employed in a department store
the heart transplant = the heart transplantation
to prevent: The detective prevented the boy from running away.
afterwards: One always knows better after the fact.
the backyard workshop: a small workshop (which is situated in the backyard of a housing complex)
the boom
hundred-fold: Hundreds of car thefts occur.
the Department for Juvenile Welfare
the Court Clerk for Juvenile Delinquency
the court officer

das Karosserieblech, -e — the metal of the car body

der Kassenzettel, — — the register receipt

das Kaufhaus, -̈er — the department store

klauen A (umgangssprachlich für: stehlen): Wer hat dein Fahrrad geklaut? — to **swipe** (everyday language for: to steal): Who swiped your bike?

der Kraftfahrzeugbrief, -e (= das Besitzdokument für ein Kraftfahrzeug) — the motor vehicle registration (= the official document of ownership of a motor vehicle)

kratzen: Die Kinder haben am Autolack gekratzt. — to **scratch**: The children scratched the paint on the car.

die Kripo = die Kriminalpolizei — the plainclothes police

der Kugelschreiber, — — the ball-point pen

der Kugelschreiberstand, -̈e: der Stand im Kaufhaus, wo Kugelschreiber zum Verkauf ausliegen — the shelf for ball-point pens: the shelf in a department store where ball-point pens are displayed for sale

der **Kurs**: Die Maschine nahm Kurs auf den nächsten Flugplatz. — the **course**: The airplane took its course towards the next airport.

der Lack, -e — the paint, the varnish

die Limousine, -n — the limousine

locken A: Er lockte mich aus dem Haus. — to **coax, to intice:** He coaxed me out of the house.

der Luxuswagen, — — the luxury car

die Markenbutter = die Qualitätsbutter — the brand-name butter = the butter of quality

die Messe, -n (= die Verkaufsmesse) — the fair (= the selling fair)

der Mitarbeiter, — — the colleague

mitsamt = zusammen mit — altogether = together with

der Mittelmeerhafen, -̈ — the Mediterranean port

mittels: mittels eines Nachschlüssels — by means of: with a master key

der Nachschlüssel, — — the master key

der Orient — the Orient

die Papiere (Plural) = die Dokumente — the papers = the documents

der Paragraph, -en (eines Gesetzes) — the section (of a law)

das Parkhaus, -̈er — the parking garage

die **Partei**: Mein Freund hat für mich Partei ergriffen. — the **party**: My friend took my side.

passend: bei passender Gelegenheit — appropriate(ly): at an appropriate opportunity

das Porto — the postage

der Probeaufbruch, -̈e: ein Einbruch zur Probe — the practice break-in: a burglary for practice

der Profi-Dieb, -e = der Berufsdieb (= einer, der berufsmäßig stiehlt) — the professional thief (= one who steals professionally)

das Protokoll, -e — the records, the report

der Protokollführer, — — the recorder

prüfen A: Das Gericht wird den Fall prüfen. — to **examine:** The court will examine the case.

raffiniert: ein raffinierter Trick — cunning(ly): a cunning trick

rechtswidrig: ein rechtswidriges Verhalten — illegal: an illegal act

das Regal, -e — the shelf

der Richter, —	the judge
riskant: eine riskante Sache	risky: a risky matter
der Sachbearbeiter, —	the official expert (for a particular field)
die Schlüsselnummer, -n	the number of the key
die Schnelligkeit: mit Schnelligkeit	the speed: speedily
simpel: ein simpler Trick	simple, simply: a simple trick
das Sortiment, -e: ein Sortiment Kugelschreiber	the assortment: an assortment of ball-point pens
der Sozialdienst, -e	the Department of Social Services
der Staatsanwalt, ⸚e	the public prosecutor
die Staatsanwaltschaft	the public prosecutor's office
stehlen A (er stiehlt, a, o): Der Junge hat einen Kugelschreiber gestohlen.	to **steal**: The boy stole a ball-point pen.
der Stempel, —: ein amtlicher Stempel	the stamp: an official stamp
StGB = das Strafgesetzbuch	the Penal Code
der Stil: im großen Stil	the style: in grand style
die Tat: eine strafbare Tat	the deed, the act: a punishable act
tausendfach	thousand-fold
das Taxi, -s	the taxi
der Teppich, -e	the carpet
der Trick, -s	the trick
der Typ, -en: ein Auto gleichen Typs	the type: a car of the same make
unauffällig: ein unauffälliges Benehmen	inconspicuous: inconspicuous behavior
der Verdienstausfall, ⸚e	the loss of wages
das Verfahren, — (bei Gericht)	the proceedings (in court)
die Verfolgungsjagd (auf Kriminelle)	the chase, the pursuit (of criminals)
verfügen über A: Der Wagen verfügt über einwandfreie Papiere.	to **have at one's disposal**: The car's documents were in perfect order.
die Verhandlung, -en	the trial, the proceedings, the hearing
der Verhandlungstermin, -e	the trial date
verhören A: Die Polizei verhört den Mann.	to **interrogate**: The police interrogated the man.
die Vernehmung, -en: die Vernehmung eines Zeugen	the interrogation: the interrogation of a witness
verschicken A an A: Das Protokoll wurde an die Staatsanwaltschaft verschickt.	to **send**: The records were sent to the office of the public prosecutor.
verschieben A (o, o): Das gestohlene Auto wurde über die Grenze verschoben.	to **move**: The stolen car was moved across the border.
vor/kommen (a, o): Heute sind schon zwei Diebstähle vorgekommen.	to **occur**: Two thefts have already occurred today.
das Vormundschaftsgericht, -e	the Court of Chancery
die Wache, -n = die Polizeiwache, -n	the guard, the station: the police station
der Wageneigentümer, —	the car owner
die Wagenpapiere (Plural)	the car papers
weg/nehmen A (er nimmt weg, a, o) = stehlen A	to **take away** = to steal
weiter/leiten A an A: Das Protokoll wurde an die Staatsanwaltschaft weitergeleitet.	to **forward**: The records were forwarded to the public prosecutor's office.
der Wert: der Wert einer Sache	the value: the value of a thing
wertvoll	valuable

der Wertgegenstand, ⁔e — the item of value, pl. the valuables
die Zeitschrift, -en — the magazine
der Zeuge, -n — the witness
zufällig: Ich habe den Diebstahl zufällig beobachtet. — **accidental, accidentally:** I observed the theft by chance.
zufolge D: der Zeitschrift „Motorwelt" zufolge ... — **according to:** According to the magazine "Motor World" ...
die Zulassungsstelle, -n (für Kraftfahrzeuge) — the Department of Registration (of motor vehicles)

Abschnitt 14

ab/lösen A: Auf der Reise hat mich meine Frau am Steuer abgelöst. — to **relieve:** During the trip my wife sometimes took over at the wheel.
ab/sichern A: Bei einer Panne auf der Landstraße muß der Wagen durch ein Warndreieck abgesichert werden. — to **secure:** If the car breaks down on the road, it has to be blocked off by a warning sign.
die Absicherung: die finanzielle Absicherung im Alter — the security: the financial security in old age
ab/warten: Warten wir ab, was geschieht! — to **wait:** Let's wait and see!
die Anfahrt zum Ferienort — the drive to the vacation destination
auf/brühen A: Soll ich einen Kaffee aufbrühen? — to **brew:** Shall I make some coffee?
auf/mucken: Als ich nicht mehr spielen wollte, muckten meine Kinder auf. — to **complain:** My children complained when I didn't want to play anymore.
aus/breiten A: Breiten Sie die Decke aus! — to **spread out:** Spread out the cover!
der **Ausdruck:** Wir sind nicht so dumm, wie es bei diesem Test zum Ausdruck kommt. — the **expression:** We are not as stupid as this test would have us be.
aus/radieren A: Radieren Sie den Fehler aus! — to **erase:** Erase the mistake!
der Bausparvertrag, ⁔e — the savings account for house construction
befriedigen A: Mein Beruf befriedigt mich. — to **satisfy:** My profession is satisfying to me.
sich **behelfen** mit (er behilft sich mit, a, o): Womit können Sie sich behelfen, wenn Ihr Blinker nicht mehr funktioniert? — to **resort to:** What can you resort to when your directional signals don't function anymore?
bejahen A: Wir bejahen die Unabhängigkeit der Frauen. — to **affirm:** We support the independence of women.
sich **betrachten:** Die Frau betrachtet sich im Spiegel. — to **regard o. s.:** The woman regards herself in the mirror.
das Blaulicht (bei Polizeiautos) — the flashing light (on police cars)
das **Dasein:** Wir Frauen sind mit unserem Dasein nicht zufrieden. — the **existence, the life:** We women are not content with our lives.
draufgängerisch: ein draufgängerischer Mann — dare-devilish: a dare-devil
sich **ducken:** Der Dieb duckte sich hinter dem Ladentisch. — to **duck:** The thief ducked behind the counter.

dumm	stupid
der Dummkopf, ⸚e	the blockhead
die Dunkelhaft	the confinement in the dark
eher: Ich bin eher vorsichtig als draufgängerisch.	rather: I am more likely to be cautious than dare-devilish.
die Eigenverantwortung	the responsibility for oneself
ein/frieren: Das Kühlwasser friert bei Frost ein.	to freeze: The cooling water freezes at below zero temperatures.
die Einzelhaft	the solitary confinement
die Erfahrung, -en	the experience
erfahrungsgemäß	empirical(ly), as experience shows
erstrebenswert: ein erstrebenswerter Beruf	worthwhile: a worthwhile profession
die Fahrbahnmarkierung (auf der Straße)	the lane division stripes (on the street)
der Ferienort, -e	the vacation place
der Filter, —	the filter
flicken A: Wir müssen das Loch flicken.	to mend, to patch up: We have to patch up the hole.
die Frauenzeitschrift, -en	the women's magazine
freiberuflich: Mein Mann ist freiberuflich tätig.	self-employed: My husband is self-employed.
die Geldanlageform, -en	the kind of financial investment
gelten als (er gilt als, a, o): Dieser Beruf gilt als erstrebenswert.	to be considered (as): This profession is considered worthwhile.
die Gesamtpunktzahl (bei einem Test)	the total number of points (in a test)
das Heftpflaster, —	the band-aid
hoch: ein hohes Alter	high: an advanced age
das Holz	the wood
der Humor	the humor
hupen: Hier ist Hupen verboten.	to honk: Honking is prohibited here.
der Kaffeefilter, —	the coffee filter
kochen: Das Wasser kocht schon.	to boil: The water is already boiling.
das Kühlwasser (im Auto)	the cooling water (in the car)
lachen: Sie werden lachen! (hier: Sie werden sich wundern.)	to laugh: You'll laugh! (here: You'll be surprised.)
die Laufbahn (in einem Beruf)	the career (in a profession)
leistungsorientiert: die leistungsorientierte Jugend	achievement oriented: achievement oriented youth
löschen: Löschen Sie bitte das Licht!	to turn out: Please turn out the light.
der Luftfilter, —	the air filter
mangelhaft: mangelhafte Leistungen	insufficient(ly): unsatisfactory achievements
merken A: Ich habe nicht gemerkt, daß ...	to notice: I didn't notice that ...
die Mittellinie, -n (als Straßenmarkierung)	the middle line (as a street marking)
morsch: morsches Holz	rotten: rotten wood
mühevoll: mühevolle Arbeit	laborious: laborious work
die Mullbinde, -n	the muslin bandage
nüchtern: Der Mann ist vollkommen nüchtern. Er hat keinen Alkohol getrunken.	sober: The man is totally sober. He has consumed no alcohol.
die Panne, -n	the break-down
der Punkt, -e (bei einem Test)	the point (in a test)

quer/stellen A: Die Polizei stellte ihren Wagen quer.

to **place laterally**: The police placed their car laterally across the road.

das **Roß**, ̈(ss)er: Er sitzt auf dem hohen Roß. (= Er ist überheblich.)

the **horse**: He is on his high horse. (= He is arrogant.)

rücksichtsvoll: ein rücksichtsvoller Autofahrer

considerate(ly): a considerate driver

der Rückspiegel, —

the rear-view mirror

sagenhaft (umgangssprachlich für: außerordentlich)

legendary, incredible (everyday language for: extraordinary)

der Schaden, ̈

the damage

die Scheibenwaschanlage, -n

the windshield washing system

der Scheinwerfer, —

the headlight

der Schonbezug, ̈e (auf einem Autositz)

the protective cover (on a car seat)

die Selbständigkeit

the independence

die Sirene, -n

the siren

das Sparbuch, ̈er

the savings account

der **Spaß**, ̈e: Die Polizei versteht keinen Spaß.

the **joke**: The police don't have a sense of humor.

der Spott

the ridicule

stammen aus: Der Artikel stammt aus einer Zeitschrift.

to **come from**: The article comes from a magazine.

statistisch

statistical(ly)

stockbetrunken = total betrunken

dead drunk = totally drunk

der Straßenrand, ̈er

the shoulder of the road

die Tätigkeit, -en

the activity, the job

das Testergebnis, -se

the test results

überwiegend: Frauen fahren überwiegend rücksichtsvoller als Männer.

predominant(ly): On the whole women drive more considerately than men.

um/gehen können: Du kannst nicht mit Geld umgehen.

to **be able to deal with:** You can't handle money.

die Unabhängigkeit

the independence

unauffällig = ohne aufzufallen

inconspicuous(ly) = without attracting attention

sich **unsicher** zeigen: Er zeigt sich beim Autofahren noch sehr unsicher.

to **be insecure:** He is still very insecure in driving a car.

die Untersuchung, -en

the research, the investigation, the study

sich **verhalten** (er verhält sich, ie, a): Wie verhalten Sie sich bei einer Panne?

to **behave:** How do you conduct yourself in case of a break-down?

vernünftig: eine vernünftige Ansicht

reasonable, reasonably: a reasonable opinion

die Versorgung (im Alter)

the provision (in old age)

vertuschen A: Man wollte den Diebstahl vertuschen.

to **hide, to conceal:** They wanted to conceal the theft.

verzichten auf: Ich verzichte heute auf Kaffee.

to **forego:** I'm passing up coffee today.

für **voll** nehmen A: Viele Männer nehmen die Frauen nicht für voll.

to **take seriously:** Many men don't take women seriously.

vordringlich: eine vordringliche Aufgabe

urgent: an urgent task

vor/legen A: Darf ich Ihnen einen Test vorlegen?

to **put before:** Would you mind taking this test?

die Vorstellung, -en: Welche Vorstellungen haben Sie über Ihren künftigen Beruf?

the idea: What ideas do you have about your future profession?

das Warndreieck, -e

the warning sign

witzig: eine witzige Antwort

funny: a funny answer

zauberhaft = wunderbar: eine zauberhafte Frau

enchanting = wonderful: an enchanting woman

zweifelhaft: ein zweifelhaftes Geschäft

dubious(ly): a shady business

zwingen A zu (a, u): Der Polizist hat mich gezwungen anzuhalten.

to force: The policeman forced me to stop.

Abschnitt 15

ab/fordern A: Den Sportlern wird das Letzte abgefordert, damit sie siegen.

to demand: The utmost is demanded from athletes, so that they win.

abgestellt: Das Programm ist ganz auf die Interessen unserer Gäste abgestellt.

designed for: The program is designed entirely to suit the interests of our guests.

abgetragene Kräfte = verbrauchte Kräfte

worn-out energies = used-up energies

ab/winken: Als ich ihn fragte, ob er kommen wolle, winkte er gleich ab.

to decline: When I asked him whether he wanted to come, he immediately made a declining gesture.

albern: eine alberne Frage

silly, foolish: a silly question

die Anreise (zu einem Urlaubsort)

the drive (to a vacation place)

die Anspannung (im Beruf)

the stress (on the job)

sich an/vertrauen D: Welchem Arzt haben Sie sich anvertraut?

to entrust o. s. to, to confide: In which doctor have you confided?

auf/bauen A: Bei einer Kur können Sie Ihre Kräfte wieder aufbauen.

to build up: You can build up your strength again by visiting a spa.

auf/weisen (ie, ie): Verschiedene Nahrungsmittel weisen krebsfördernde Stoffe auf.

to show, to exhibit: Many kinds of foods contain cancer producing substances.

der Ausgleich

the compensation

sich aus/setzen D: Wir müssen uns dem täglichen Streß aussetzen.

to expose o. s.: We have to expose ourselves to daily stress.

der Badeort, -e

the spa

die „Badereise": die Reise zu einer Kur

the "spa visit": the visit to a spa

der Ballaststoff, -e (in der Nahrung)

the roughage (in foods)

die Bauernweisheit, -en

the farmer's wisdom

beachtlich: eine beachtliche Menge

considerable, considerably: a considerable amount

der Bedarf: der tägliche Bedarf an Vitaminen

the need, the requirement: the daily requirement of vitamins

sich begnügen mit: Ich begnüge mich beim Frühstück mit einer Tasse Kaffee.

to be satisfied with: I'm satisfied with a cup of coffee for breakfast.

die Belastung, -en (im Beruf)

the burden (on the job)

benötigen A: Jeder benötigt täglich eine bestimmte Menge an Vitaminen.

to need: Everyone needs a certain quantity of vitamins every day.

bewirken A: Diese Stoffe bewirken eine gewisse Müdigkeit.

der Cholesterinspiegel (im Blut)

der Darmkrebs

die Darmträgheit

die Depression, -en

deutlich machen D + A: Können Sie mir die Probleme deutlich machen?

sich **drehen**: Die Erde dreht sich täglich einmal um sich selbst.

durch/atmen: Atmen Sie in der frischen Luft tief durch!

sich **eignen** als: Vollkornbrot eignet sich vorzüglich als Ballaststoff.

ein/räumen: Sie haben mit Ihrer Meinung recht, räumte er ein.

sich **ein/setzen** für: Die Ärzte setzen sich für eine gesunde Ernährung ein.

ein/wenden (a, a): Da bin ich anderer Ansicht, wandte er ein.

enthalten A (er enthält, ie, a): Die Luft in einer Stadt enthält viele schädliche Stoffe.

entschieden: Er war entschieden anderer Meinung als wir.

die Entspannung (des Körpers)

die Epoche, -n

sich **ereifern**: Die Diskussionsteilnehmer ereiferten sich immer mehr.

der Erholungsuchende, -n

der Ernährungsphysiologe, -n

ernährungsphysiologisch

aus der **Fassung** bringen lassen: Ich habe mich bei der Diskussion nicht aus der Fassung bringen lassen.

das Fett, -e

fettreich: eine fettreiche Kost

die Fettzufuhr (in den Körper)

fehlen D: Mir fehlt nichts. — Was fehlt Ihnen?

die Flucht aus dem Alltag

sich **fühlen**: Wie fühlen Sie sich?

die Geborgenheit

der **Gehalt**: Die Luft weist einen Gehalt an Benzpyren auf.

der Geist

gelten (er gilt, a, o): Die alte Bauernweisheit gilt noch heute.

das Gemüse

---

to **cause**: These substances cause a certain fatigue.

the cholesterol content (in the blood)

cancer of the intestines

the indigestion

the depression

to **clarify**: Can you clarify the problems for me?

to **turn**: The earth revolves around itself three times a day.

to **breathe deeply**: Breathe deeply in the fresh air!

to **be suited**: Whole grain bread is an excellent roughage.

to **concede**: Your opinion is correct, he conceded.

to **promote**: Doctors encourage healthy eating habits.

to **object**: I am of another opinion, he objected.

to **contain**: The air in a city contains many harmful substances.

decided(ly): His opinion was decidedly different than ours.

the relaxation (of the body)

the epoch

to **become excited**: The participants in the discussion became more and more excited.

the person who seeks rest and relaxation

the physiologist of nutrition

based on nutritional physiology

to **become disconcerted**: I didn't let myself become disconcerted during the discussion.

the fat, the grease

fatty, greasy: greasy food

the intake of fat (into the body)

to **be lacking**: Nothing's wrong with me. — What's wrong with you?

the escape from the everyday routine

to **feel**: How do you feel?

the security

the **content, the amount**: There is a benzpyrene content in the air.

the mind

to **be valid**: The old farmer's wisdom is still valid today.

the vegetable

gesundheitsschädlich	unhealthy, harmful to health
gesundheitszerstörend	devastating to health
gleichgültig: Das ist mir gleichgültig.	**indifferent(ly):** I couldn't care less.
gravierend: ein gravierender Mangel	grave, serious: a serious deficiency
sich **halten** an A (er hält sich an, ie, a): Ich halte mich an die Empfehlungen des Arztes.	to **adhere to:** I adhere to the doctor's recommendations.
die Heilkräfte der Natur	the healing powers of nature
heißen: Wie heißt der Segenswunsch?	to **be called:** What is the good wish?
das Hilfsmittel, —	the means, the resource
um Himmelswillen!	for heaven's sake!
Indien	India
der Internist, -en	the doctor of internal medicine
kanzerogen = krebserzeugend	carcinogenic = cancer producing
die **Kenntnis:** Haben Sie das zur Kenntnis genommen?	the **knowledge:** Did you understand that?
die Kohlehydrate (Plural)	the carbohydrates
kohlehydratknappe Kost	food with low carbohydrate content
der Körper, —	the body
die Kur, -en	the cure, the treatment
der Kurgast, ⁓e	the spa visitor, the spa patient
lauten: Wie lautet der Text?	to **sound:** How does the text read?
letztlich	ultimately
die **Luft:** Wir gehen ein bißchen Luft schnappen.	the **air:** We're going to get a little fresh air.
der Mangel an Thiamin	the thiamine deficiency
die Mode	the fashion
sich **mokieren** über A: Viele Leute mokieren sich über uns.	to **sneer at:** Many people sneer at us.
die Müdigkeit	the fatigue
die Nachbarschaft	the neighborhood
nachweisbar: In der Luft sind Schadstoffe nachweisbar.	**traceable:** Harmful substances can be detected in the air.
nach/weisen A: Man hat in der Luft Schadstoffe nachgewiesen.	to **detect:** Harmful substances have been detected in the air.
das Nahrungsmittel, —	the food
die Neurose, -n	the neurosis
nutzbar machen für: Man hat die Heilkräfte der Natur für den Menschen nutzbar gemacht.	to **utilize:** Nature's healing powers have been made useful for mankind.
nutzen A: Wir müssen die Zeit nutzen.	to **use:** We must make use of our time.
das Öl, -e	the oil
die Parole, -n	the password
pflanzlich: pflanzliche Stoffe	pertaining to plants: plant substances
das Privileg, -ien	the privilege
der Prospekt, -e	the brochure
psychisch: psychische Krankheiten	psychological(ly): psychological diseases
reichhalt-: reichhaltige Nahrung, ein reichhaltiges Angebot	abundant, plentiful: abundant food, an extensive and varied offer
der Reiseveranstalter, —	the travel agent, the tour organizer

der Reiz, -e: ein körperlicher Reiz
the irritation: a bodily irritation

resignieren: Wir dürfen nicht resignieren.
to **resign, to give up:** We must not give up.

restlich
remaining

das Roggenbrot, -e
the rye bread

schaffen (u, a): (z. B. Vorrat)
to provide, to supply (for example, supplies)

schätzen A: Wir schätzen die Gesundheit.
to **value:** We value health.

die Scheibe, -n: eine Scheibe Brot (Wurst, Käse usw.)
the slice: a slice of bread (sausage, cheese, etc.)

schlank: eine schlanke Frau
slender: a slender woman

die Schmalkost (= eine reduzierte Kost)
the meager diet (= a reduced diet)

schnappen A: Ich möchte jetzt etwas Luft schnappen.
the **catch:** Now I'd like to catch some air.

der Segenswunsch, ⁻e
the good wish

der Speck
the bacon

das Spiegelei, -er
the fried egg

das Thiamin
thiamine

ticken: Die Zeitbombe tickt. (Vgl. die Uhr tickt.)
to **tick:** The time bomb is ticking. (Compare: The watch is ticking.)

tierisch: tierische Fette
animal, animal-like: animal fats

trotzig: Unser Kind ist sehr trotzig.
obstinate: Our child is very obstinate.

überflüssig: überflüssige Argumente
superfluous: superfluous arguments

überholt: überholte Ansichten
antiquated: antiquated views

überraschen A: Er hat mich überrascht.
to **surprise:** he surprised me.

umfänglich: ein umfänglicher Prospekt
voluminous: a voluminous brochure

umfangreich: ein umfangreiches Essen
extensive, abundant: an abundant meal

unaufhörlich: unaufhörliche Fragerei
incessant(ly): incessant questioning

unbeeindruckt: Seine Äußerungen ließen mich unbeeindruckt.
unimpressed: His remarks left me unimpressed.

ungeahnt: ungeahnte Fähigkeiten
unimagined: unimagined abilities

unlängst = vor kurzem
recently = a short time ago

unqualifiziert: unqualifizierte Bemerkungen
unqualified: unqualified remarks

die Verbundenheit mit der Natur
the bond with nature

verordnen: D + A: Der Arzt hat mir diese Medizin verordnet.
to **prescribe:** The doctor prescribed this medicine for me.

die Verschmutzung der Luft
the air pollution

die Verteufelung von politischen Ansichten anderer
the denunciation of the political views of others

das Vertrauen in die Heilkräfte der Natur
the confidence in nature's healing powers

verurteilen A: Ich muß deine Ansichten scharf verurteilen.
to **condemn:** I must condemn your views strongly.

verzichten auf A: Wer möchte schon auf ein gutes Essen verzichten?
to **renounce:** Who wants to pass up a good meal?

verzweifelt: ein verzweifelter Mensch
desperate: a desperate person

das Vollkornbrot, -e
the whole grain bread

das Vollkornprodukt, -e
the whole grain product

der **Vorrat:** Wir müssen uns einen Vorrat an Vitaminen schaffen.
the **supply:** We have to procure a supply of vitamins.

vorzüglich: ein vorzügliches Essen
exquisite: an exquisite meal